Trilogy

Drawing Art

CATS

The Art of Drawing; Portraits of Kitties Reproduced in Series for Framing

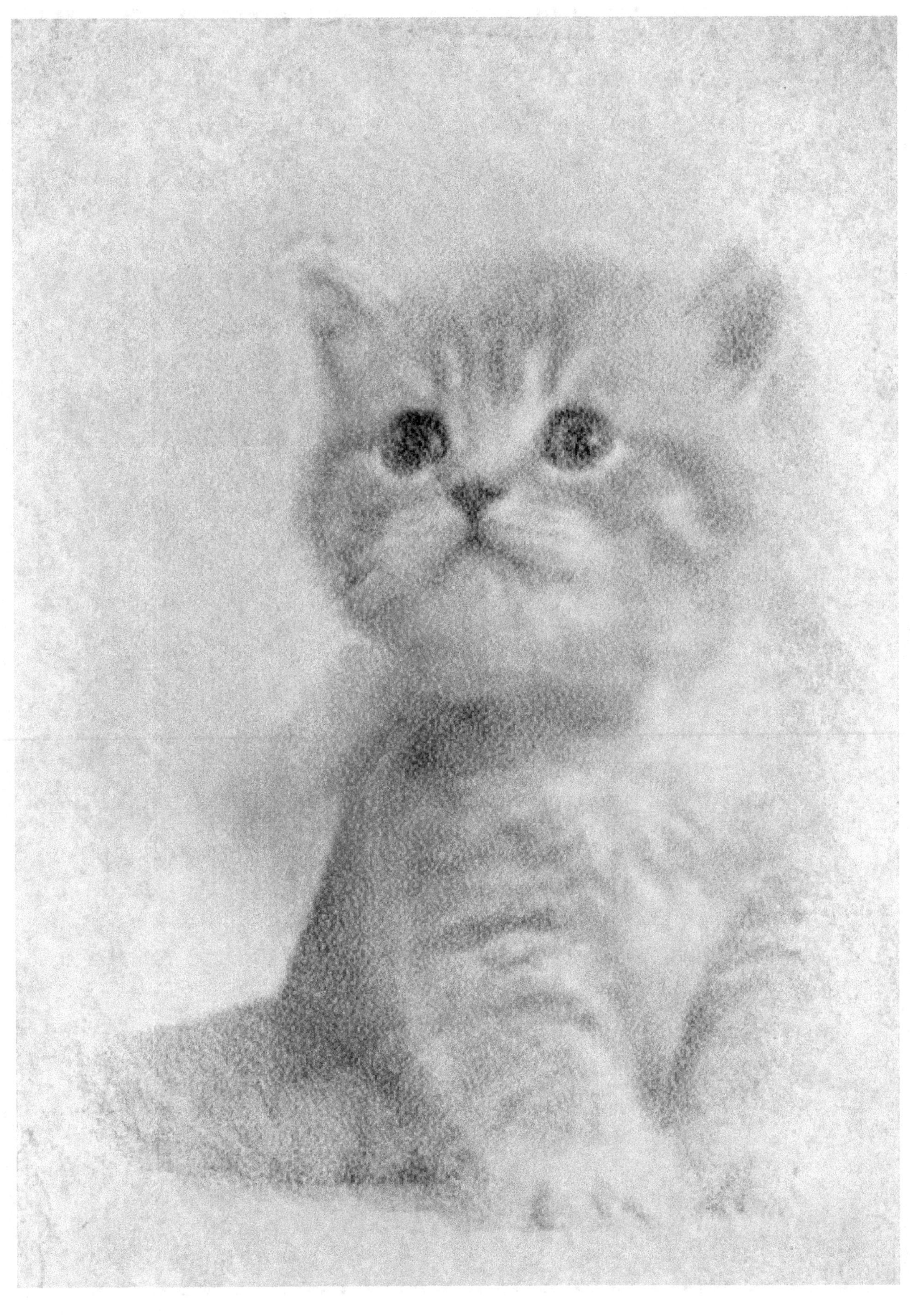

From Frame

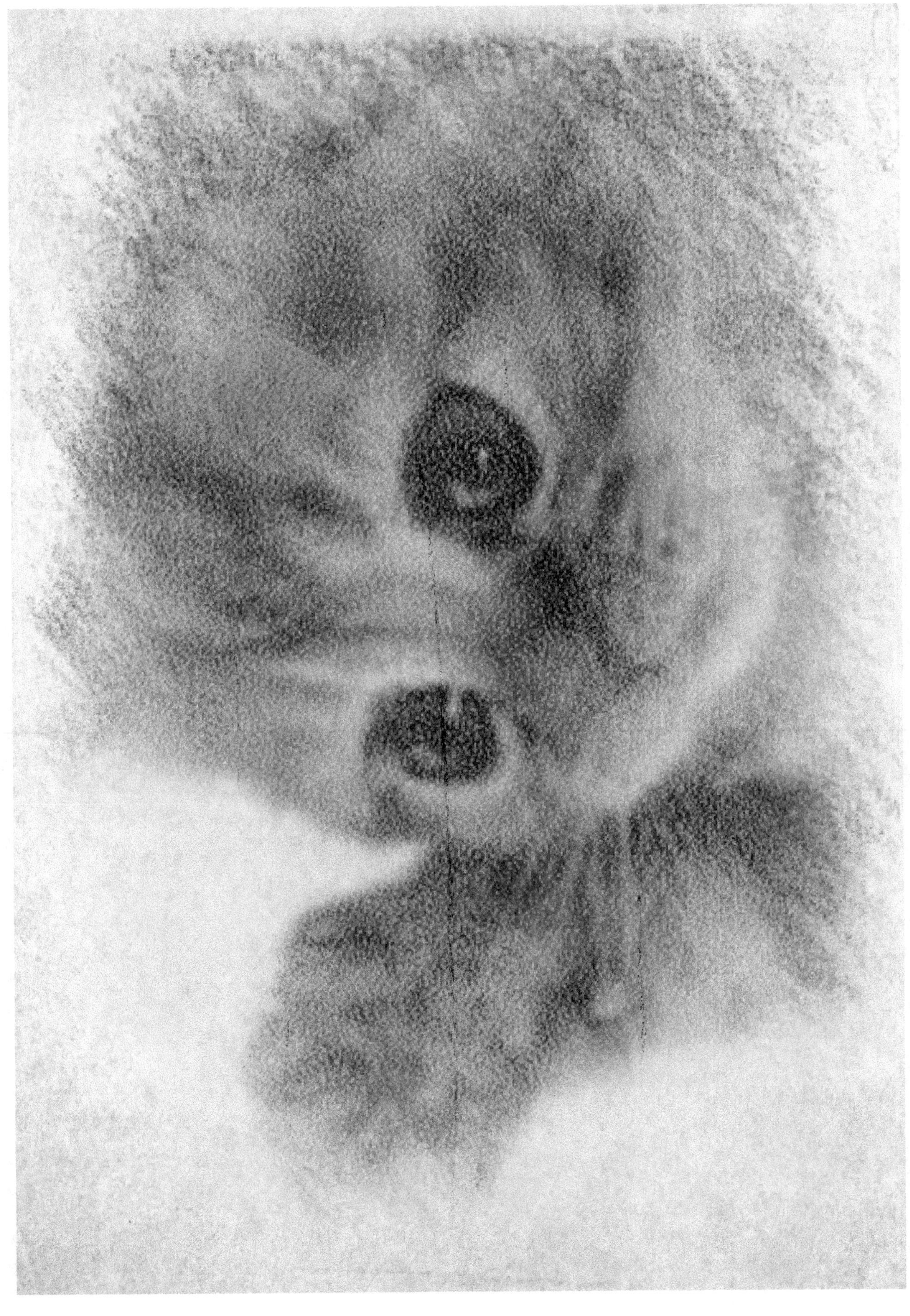

From Frame

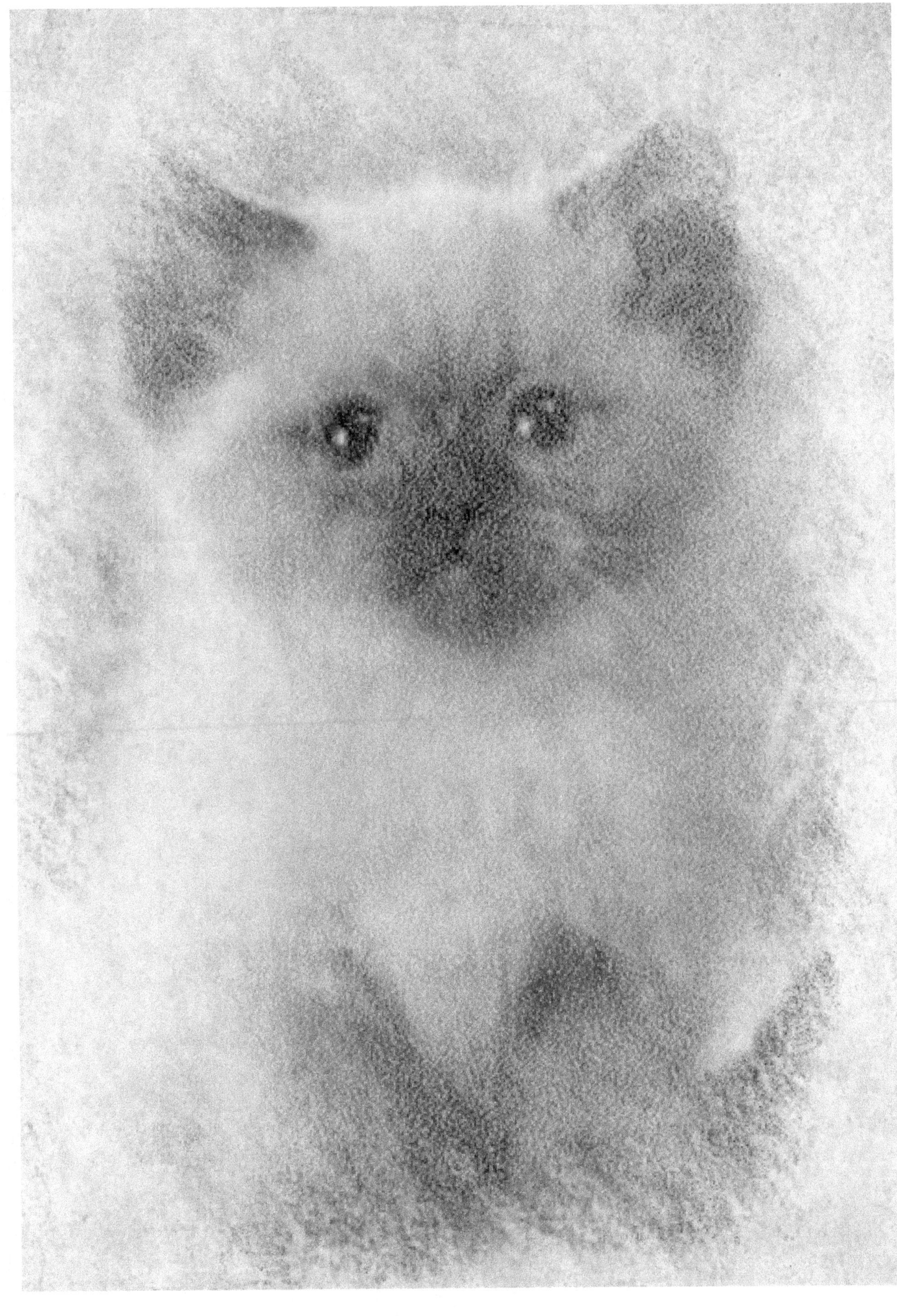

From Frame

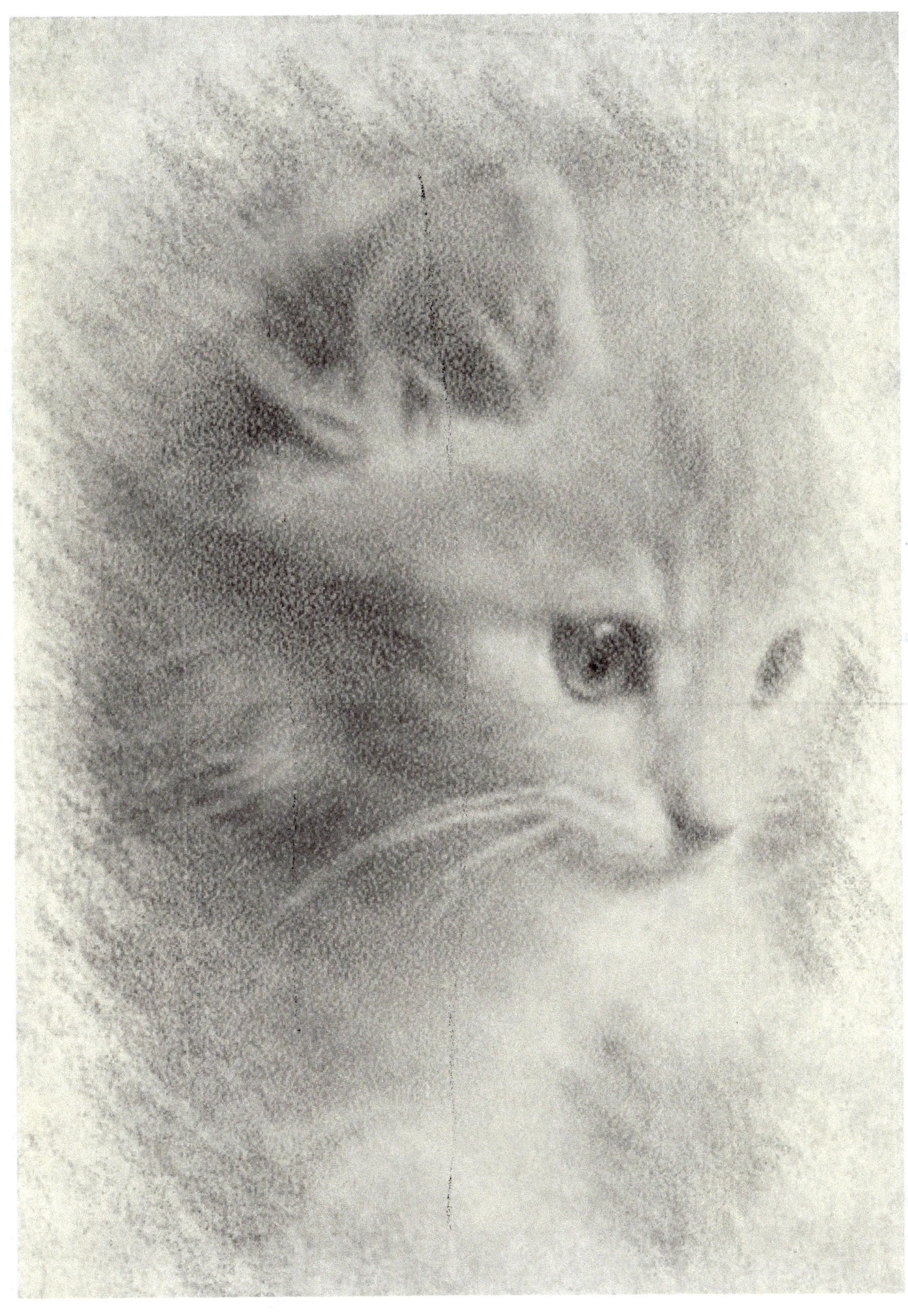

From Frame

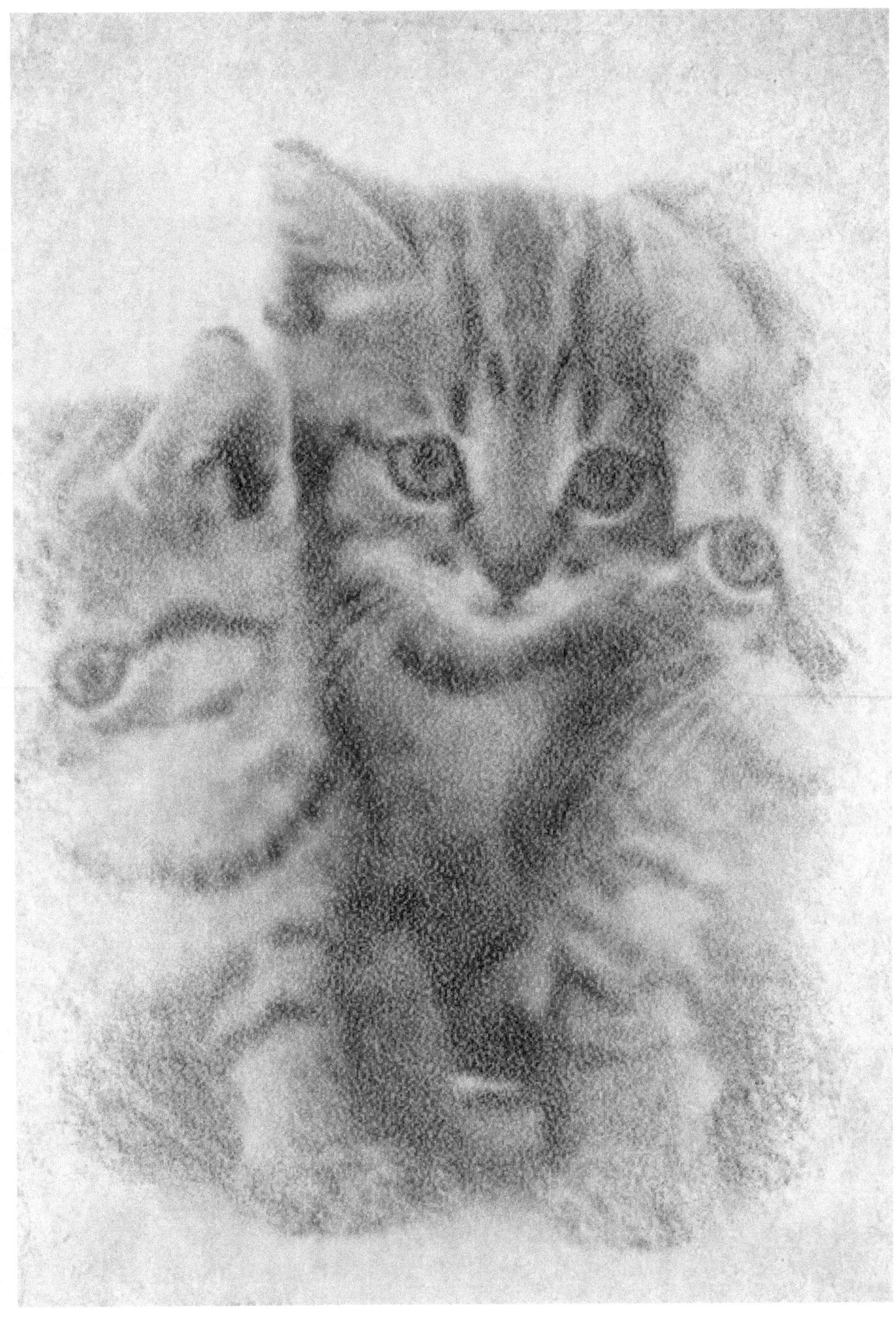

From Frame

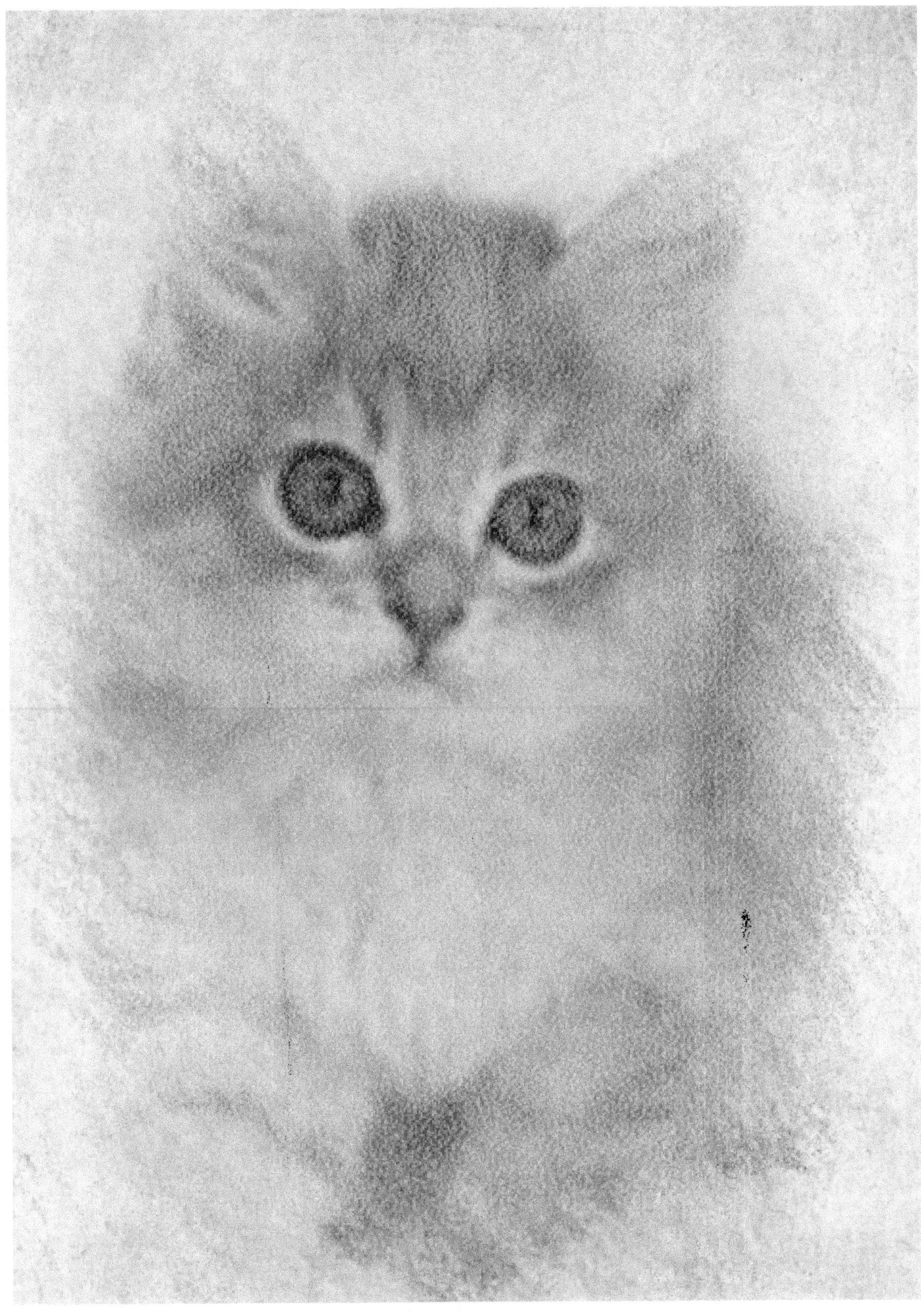

From Frame

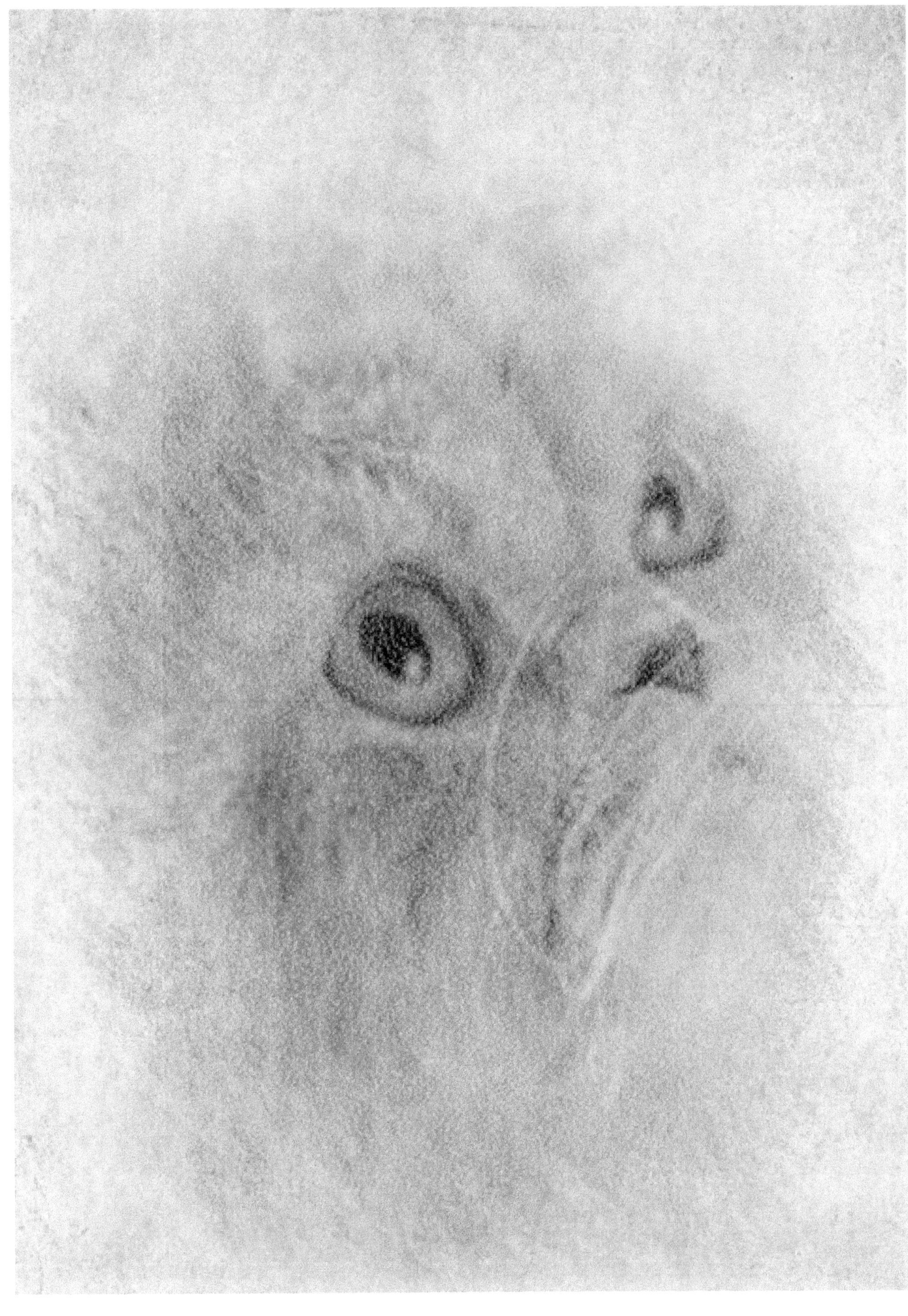

From Frame

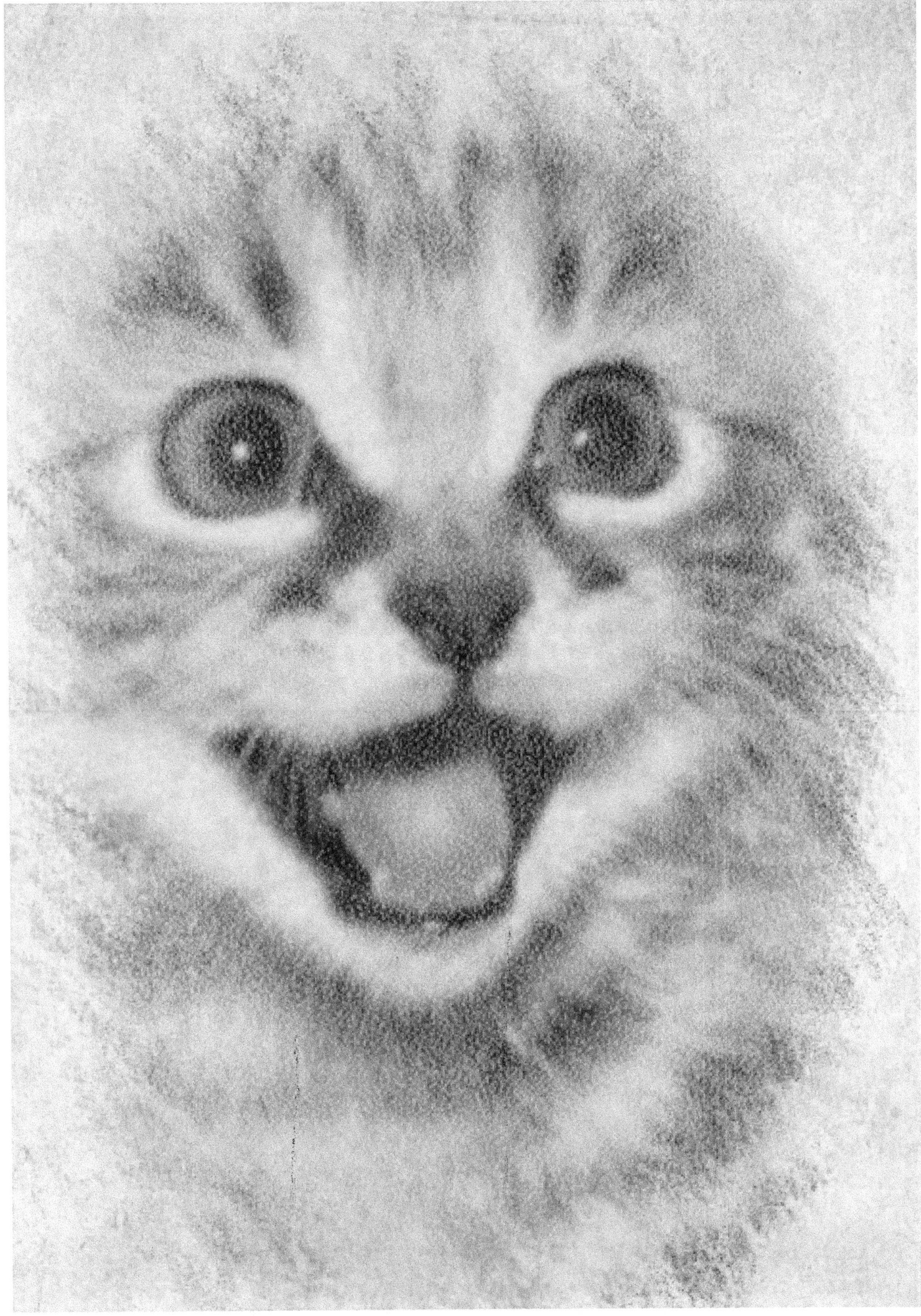

From Frame

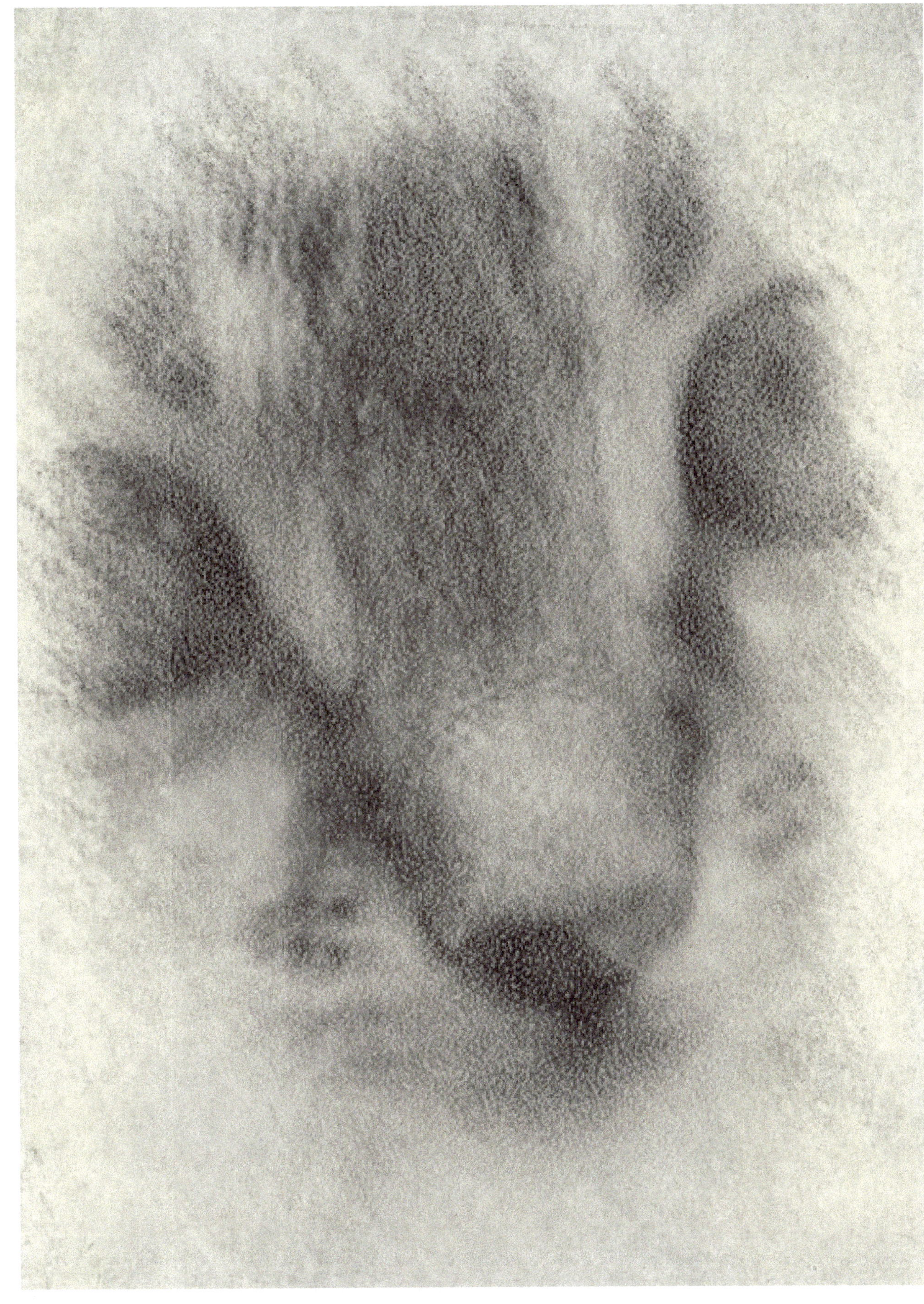

From Frame

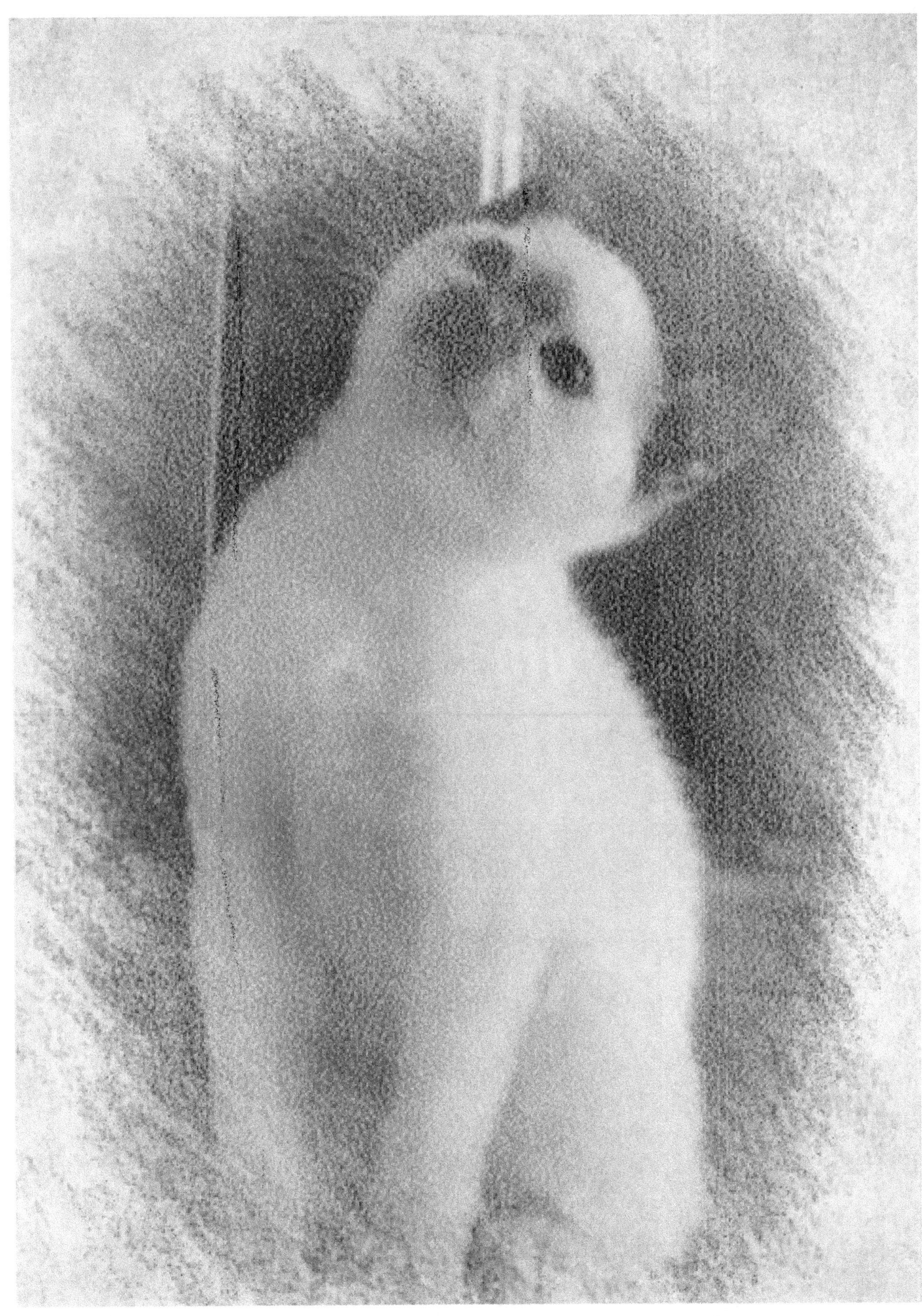

From Frame

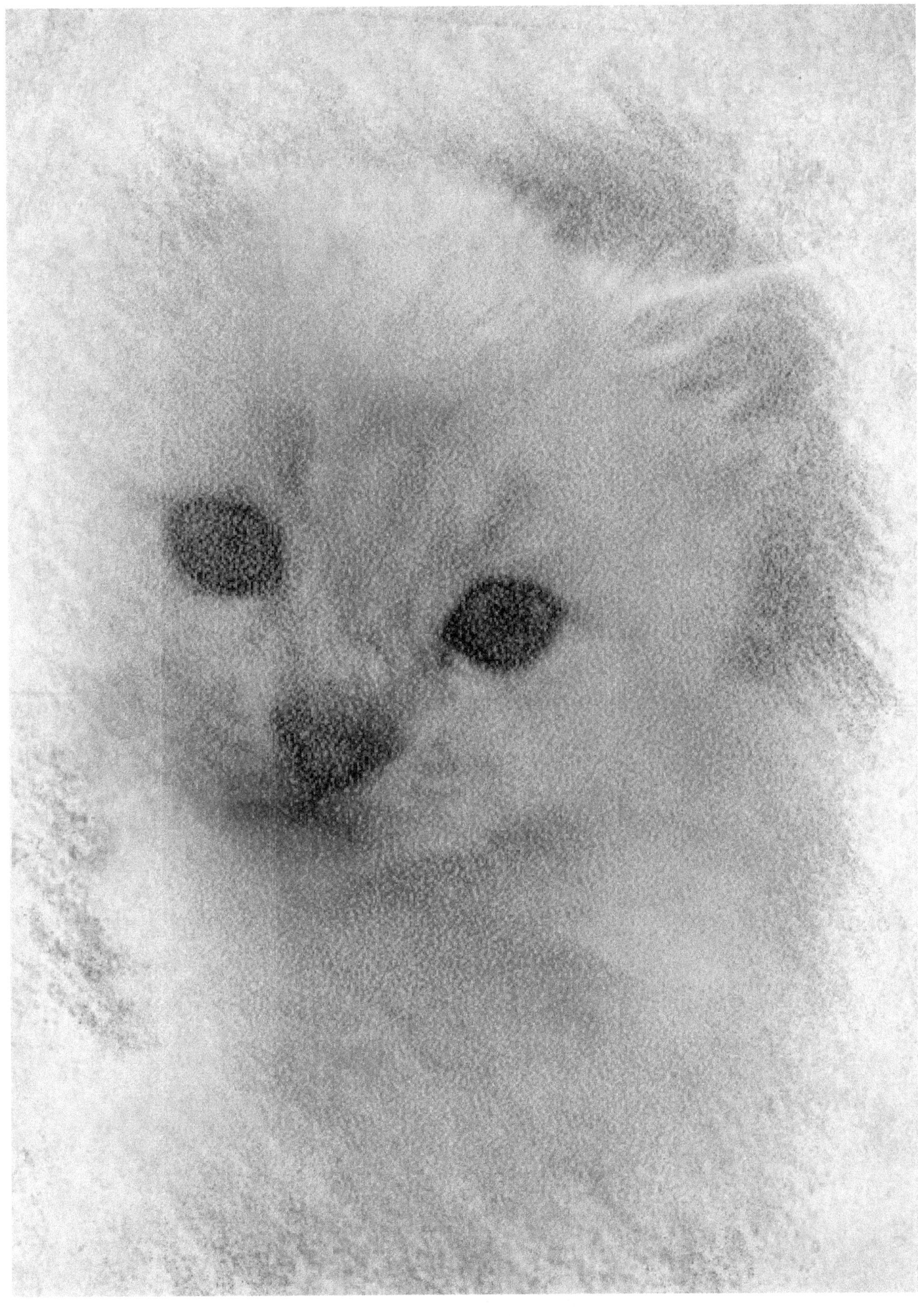

From Frame

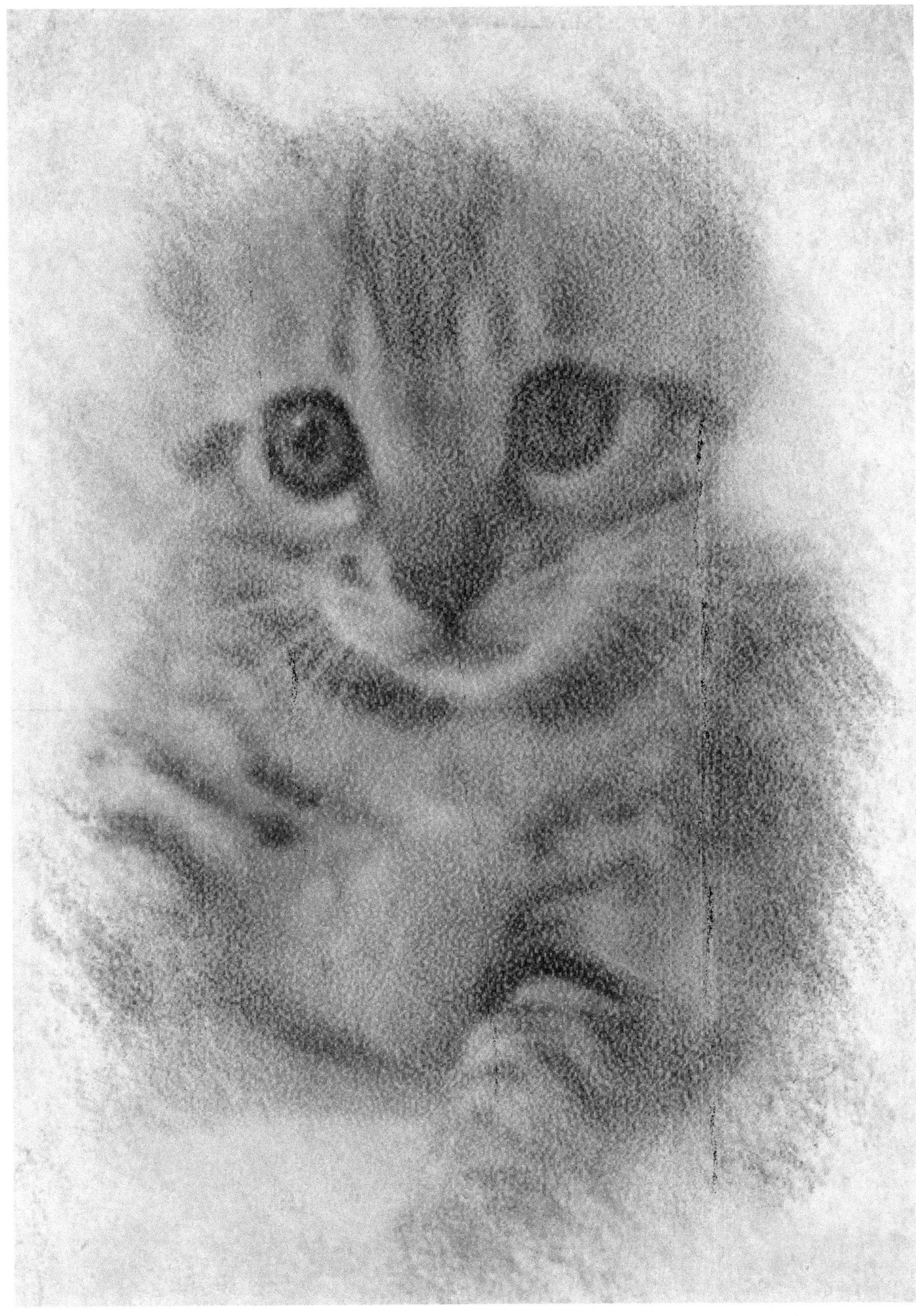

From Frame

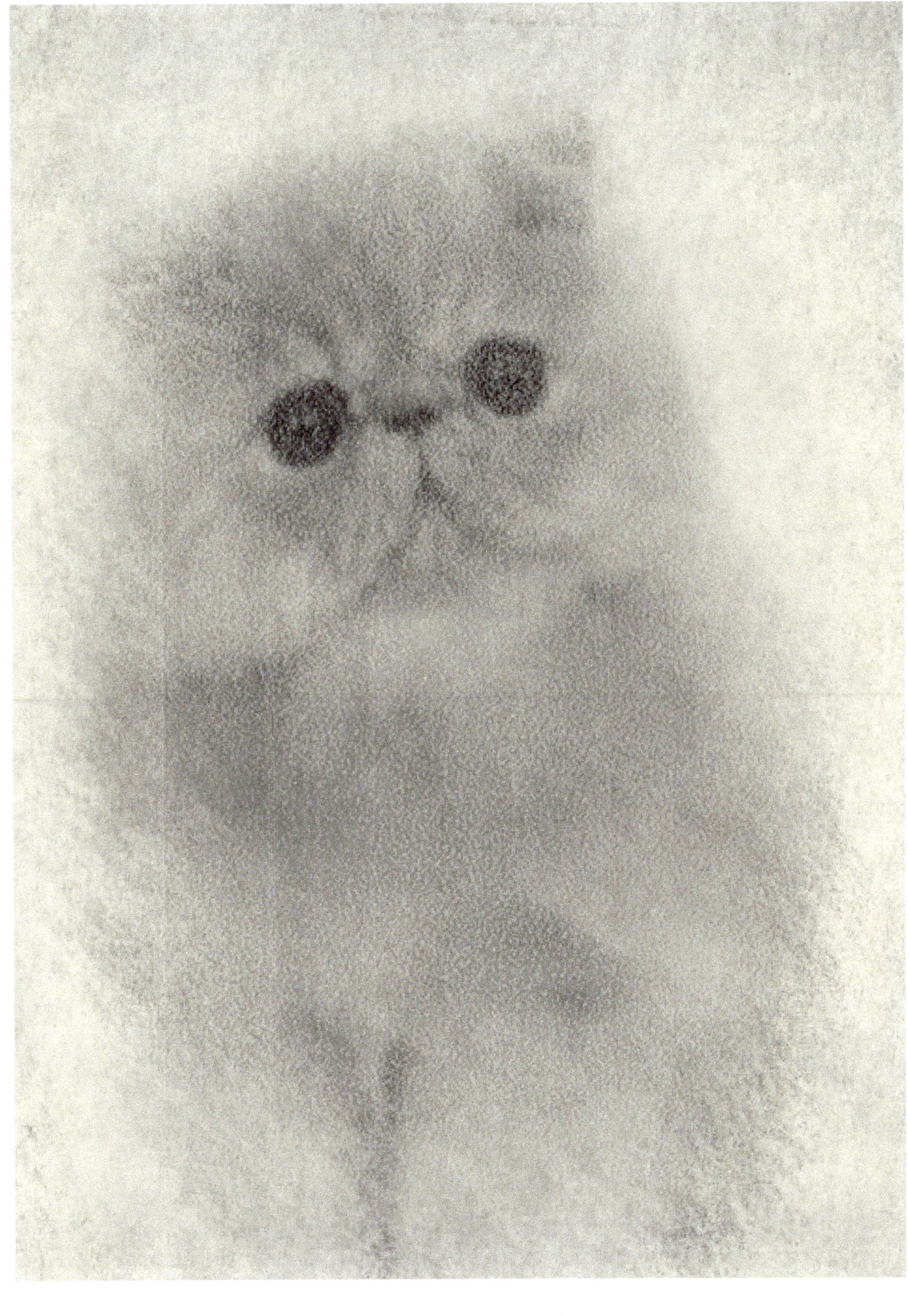

From Frame

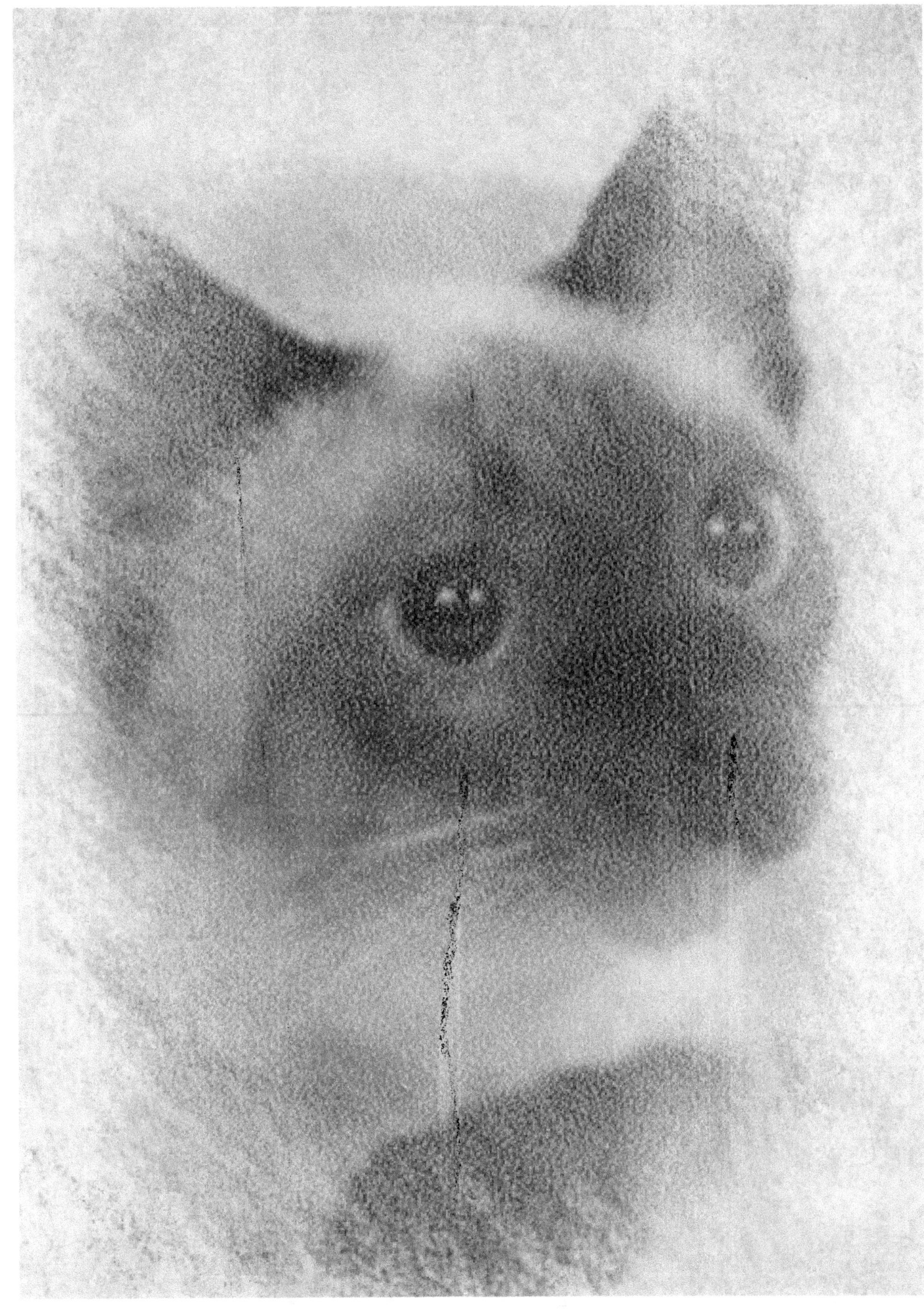

From Frame

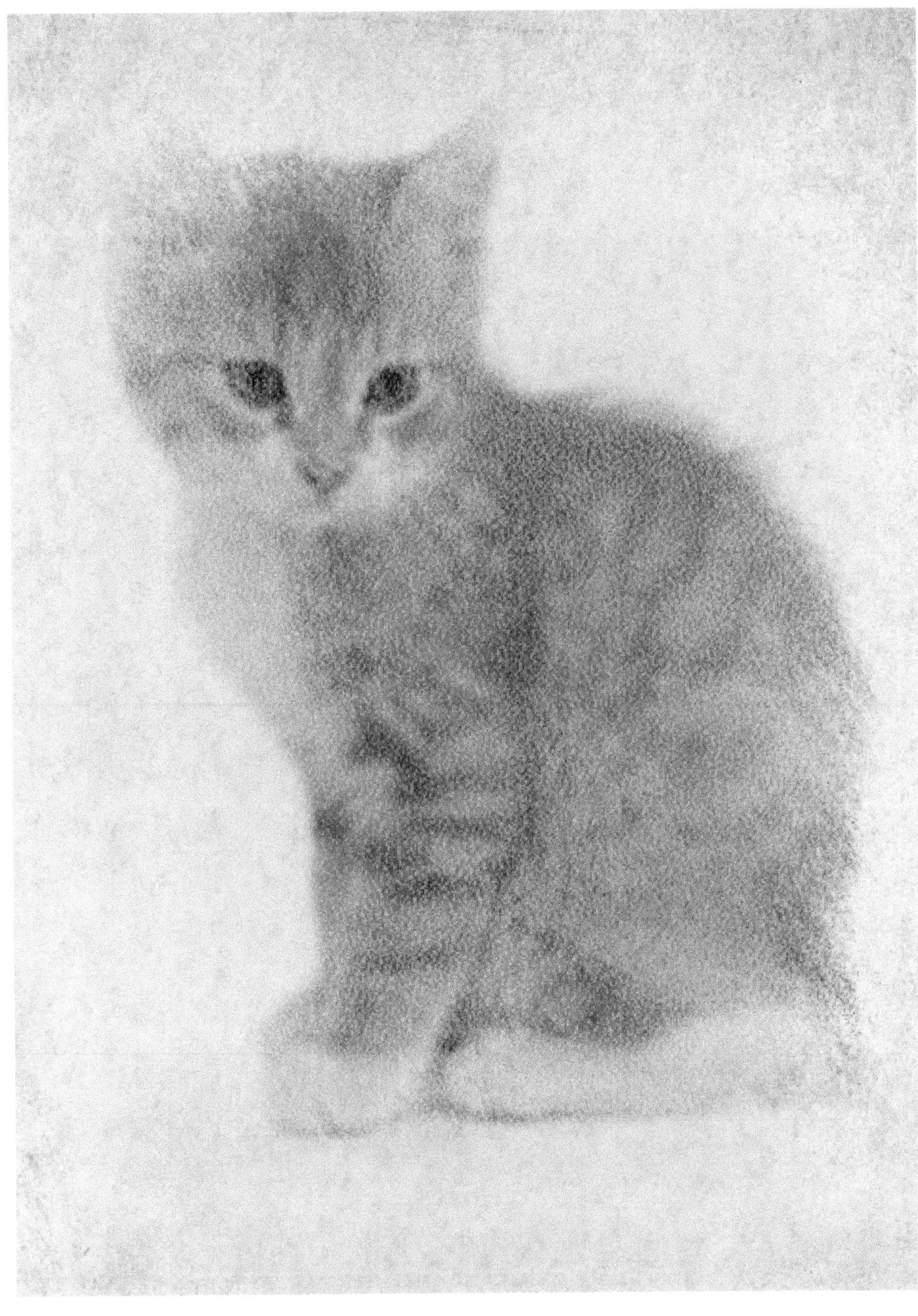

From Frame

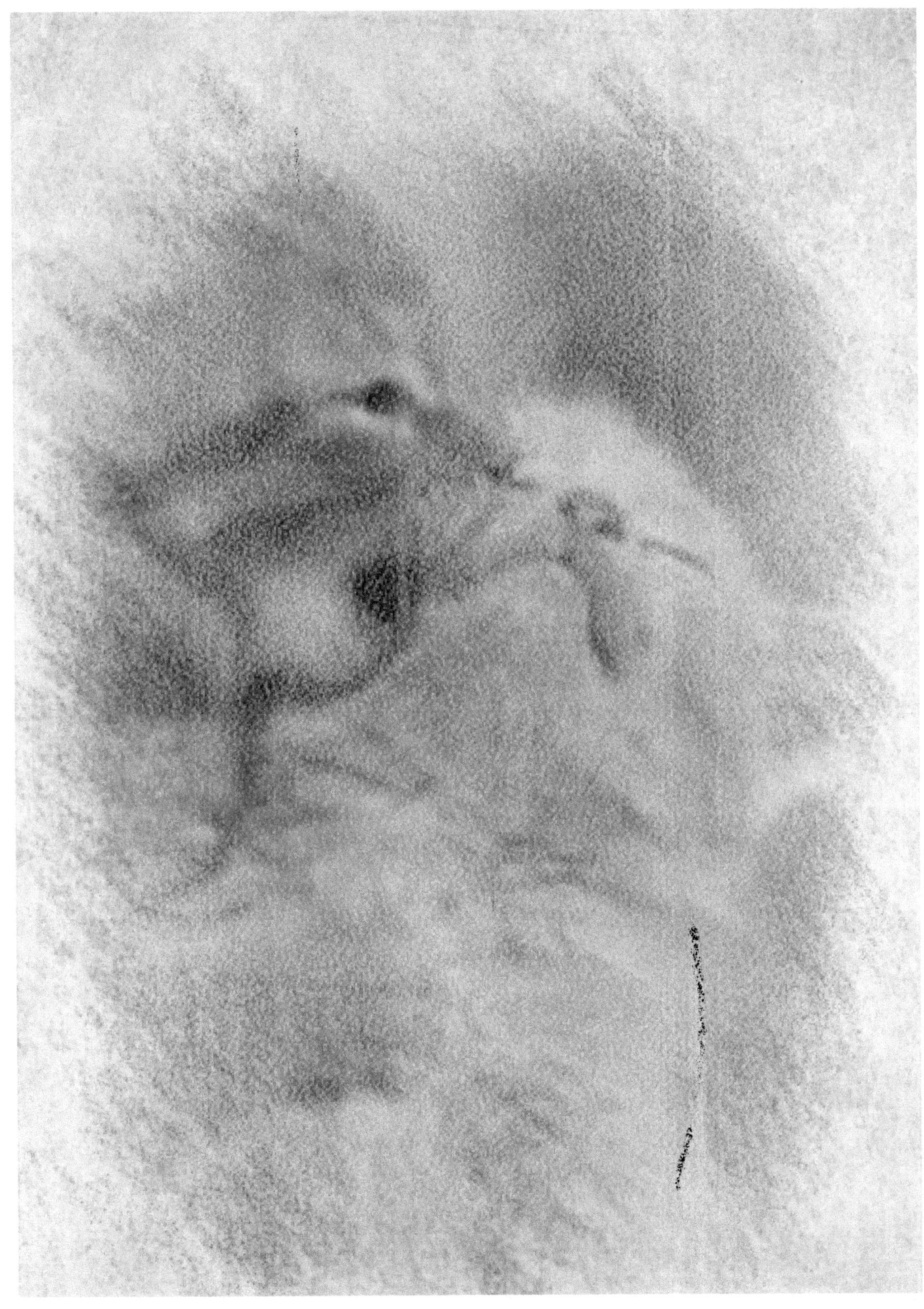

From Frame

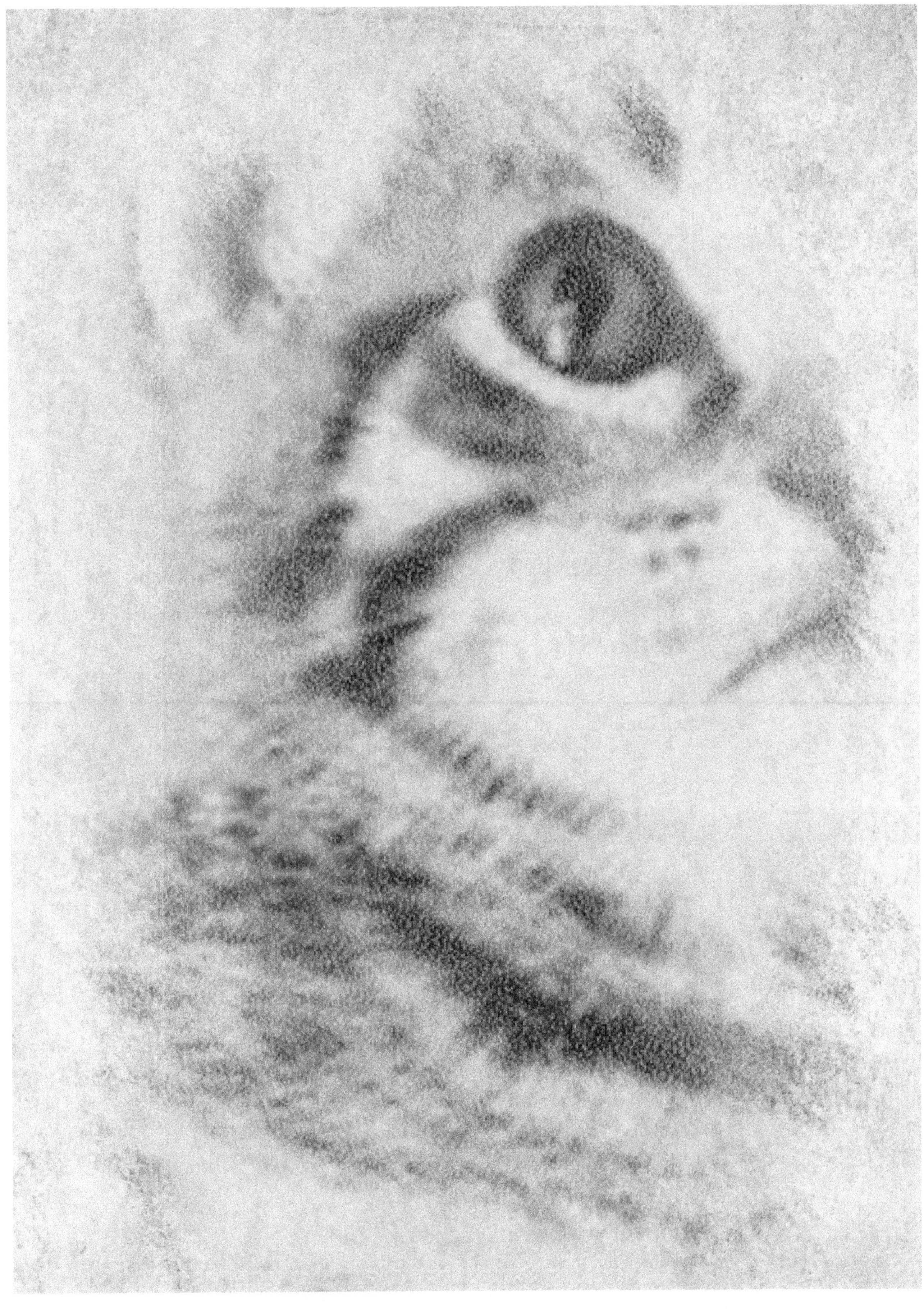

From Frame

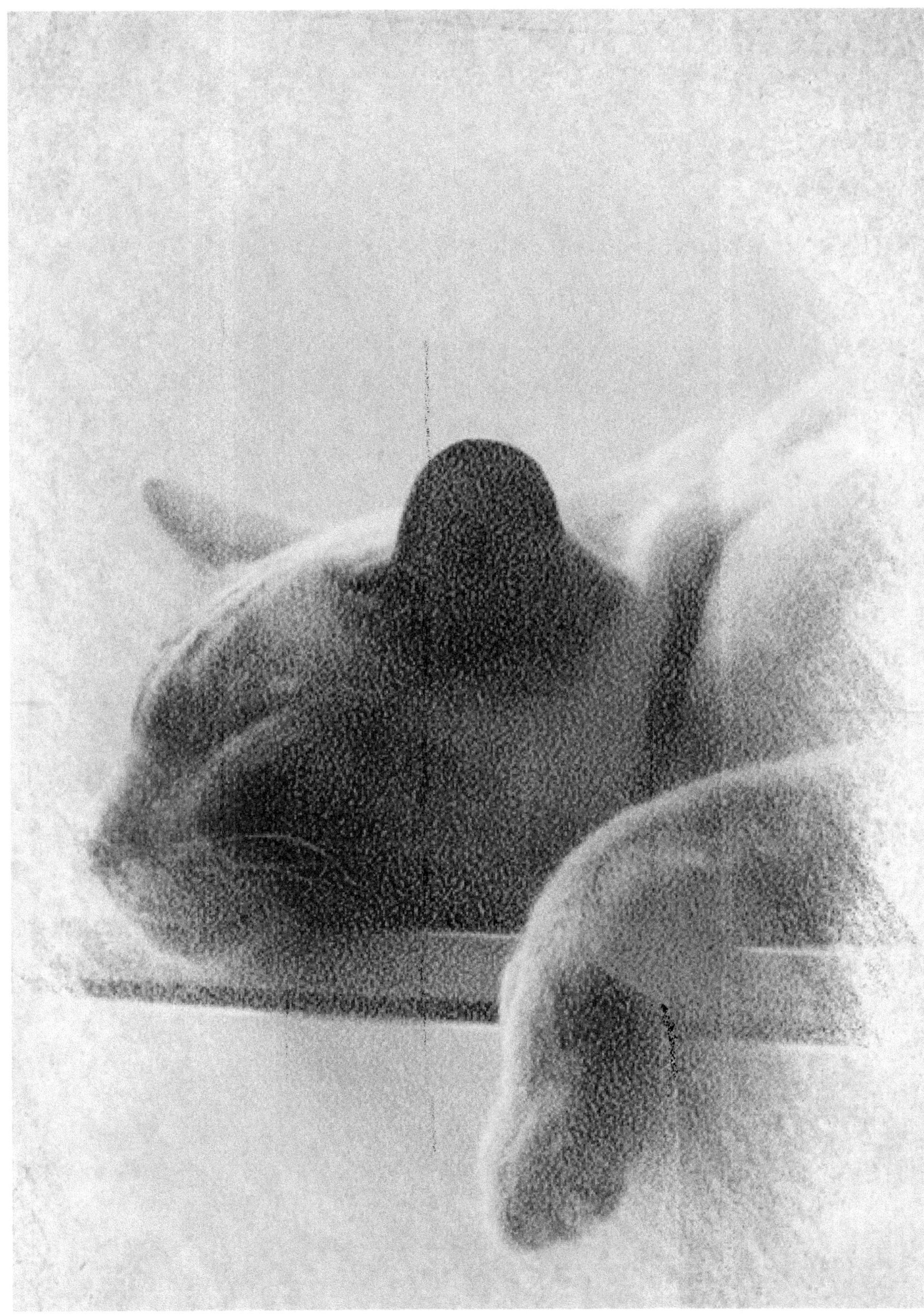

From Frame

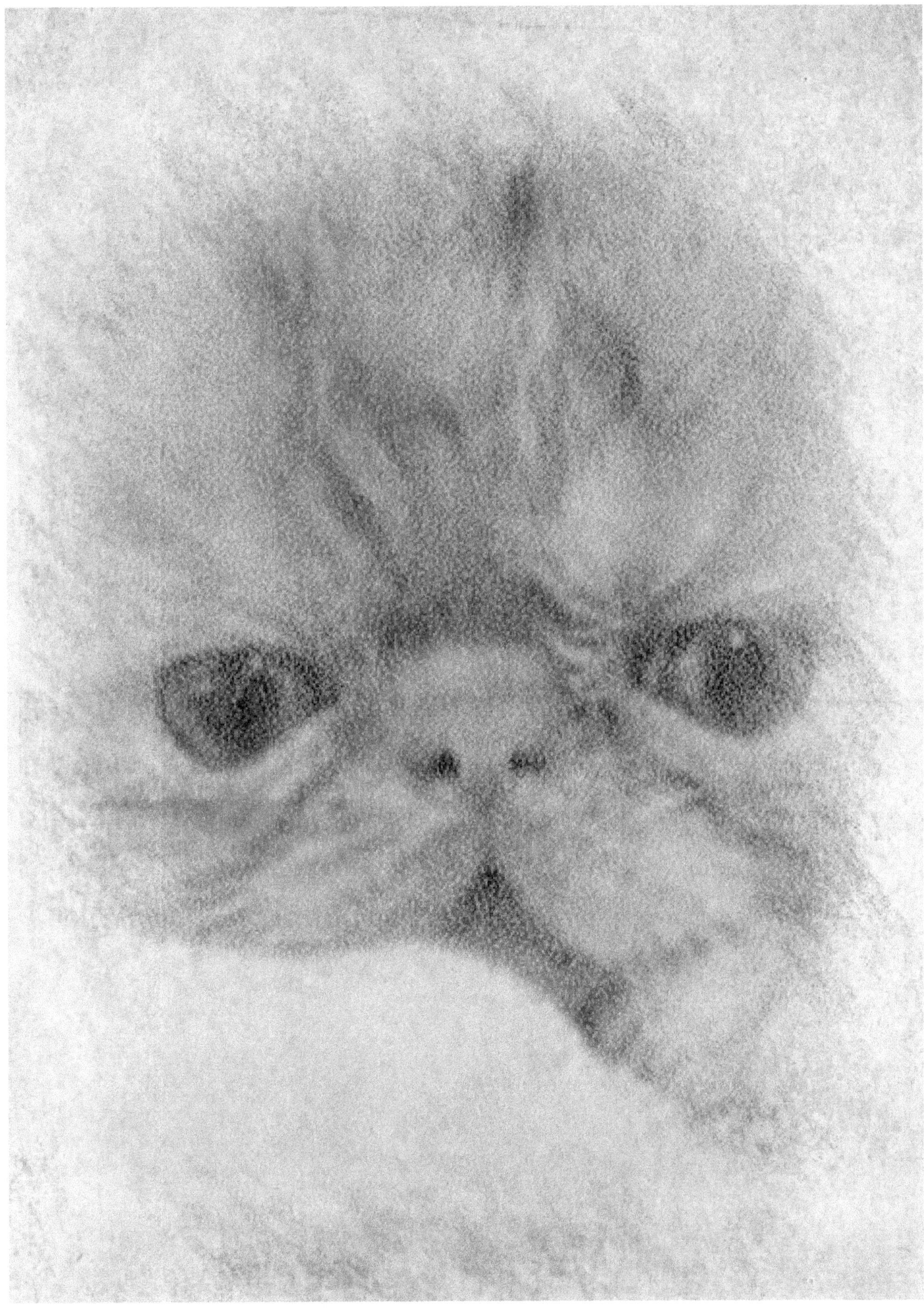

From Frame

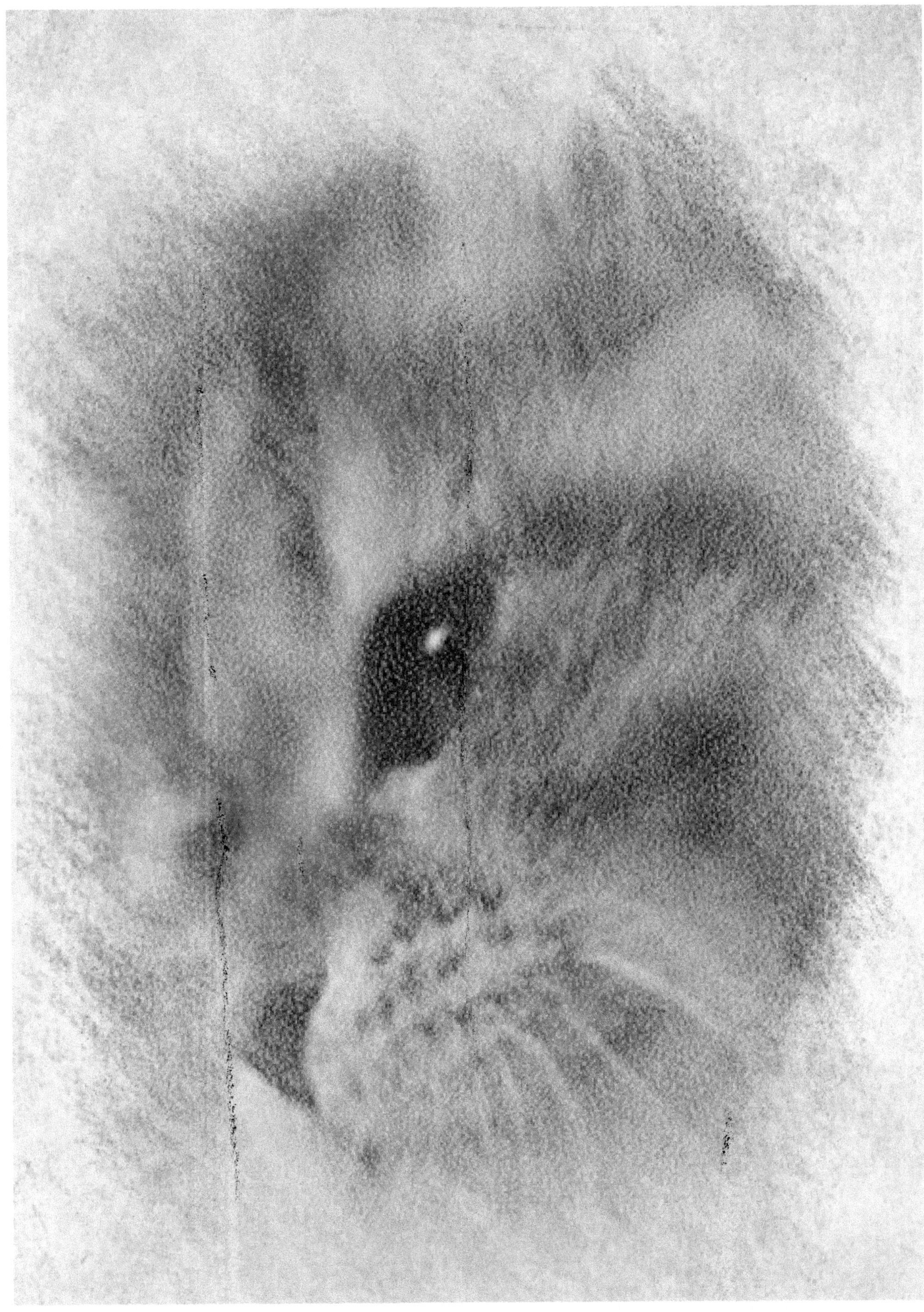

From Frame

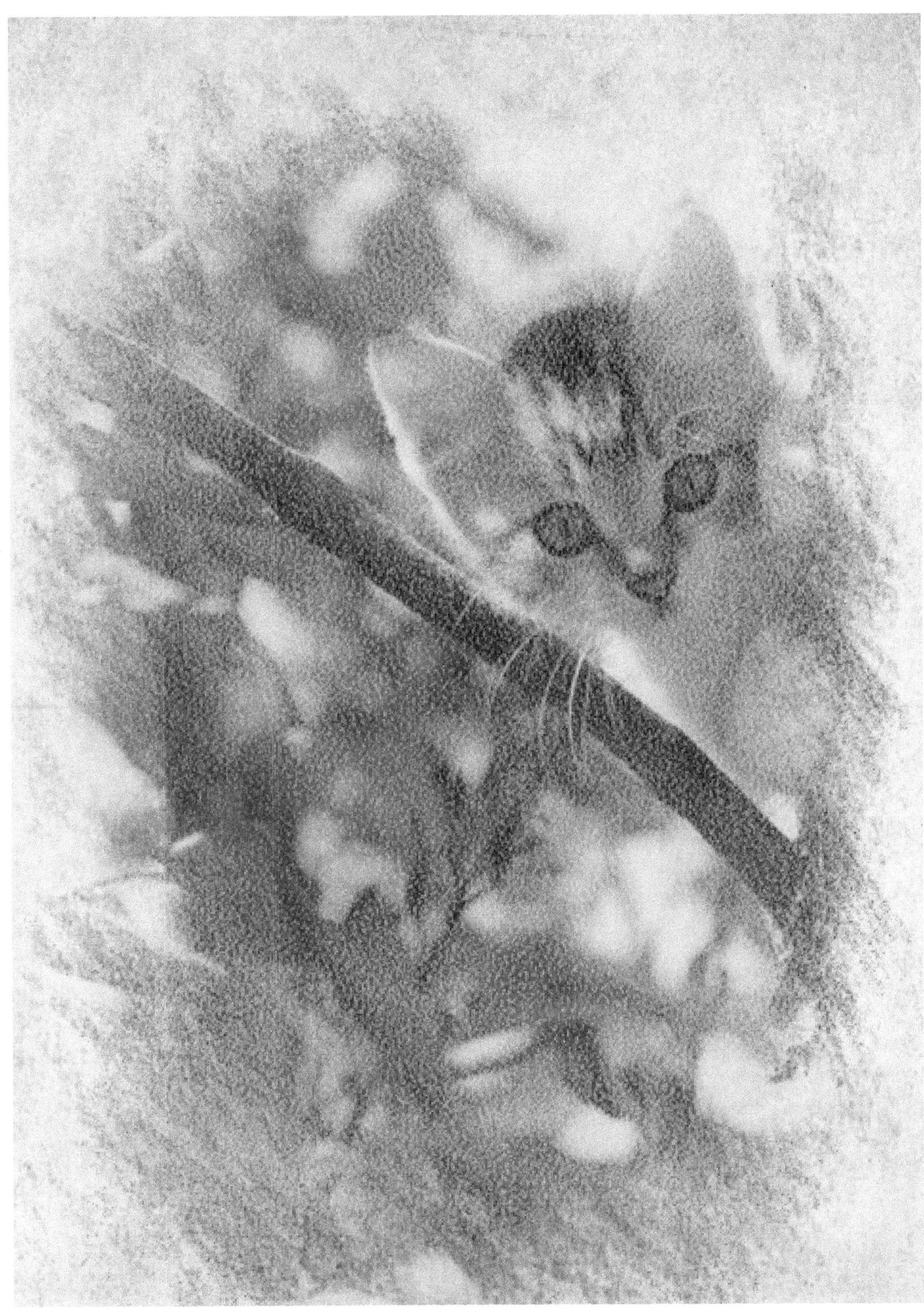

From Frame

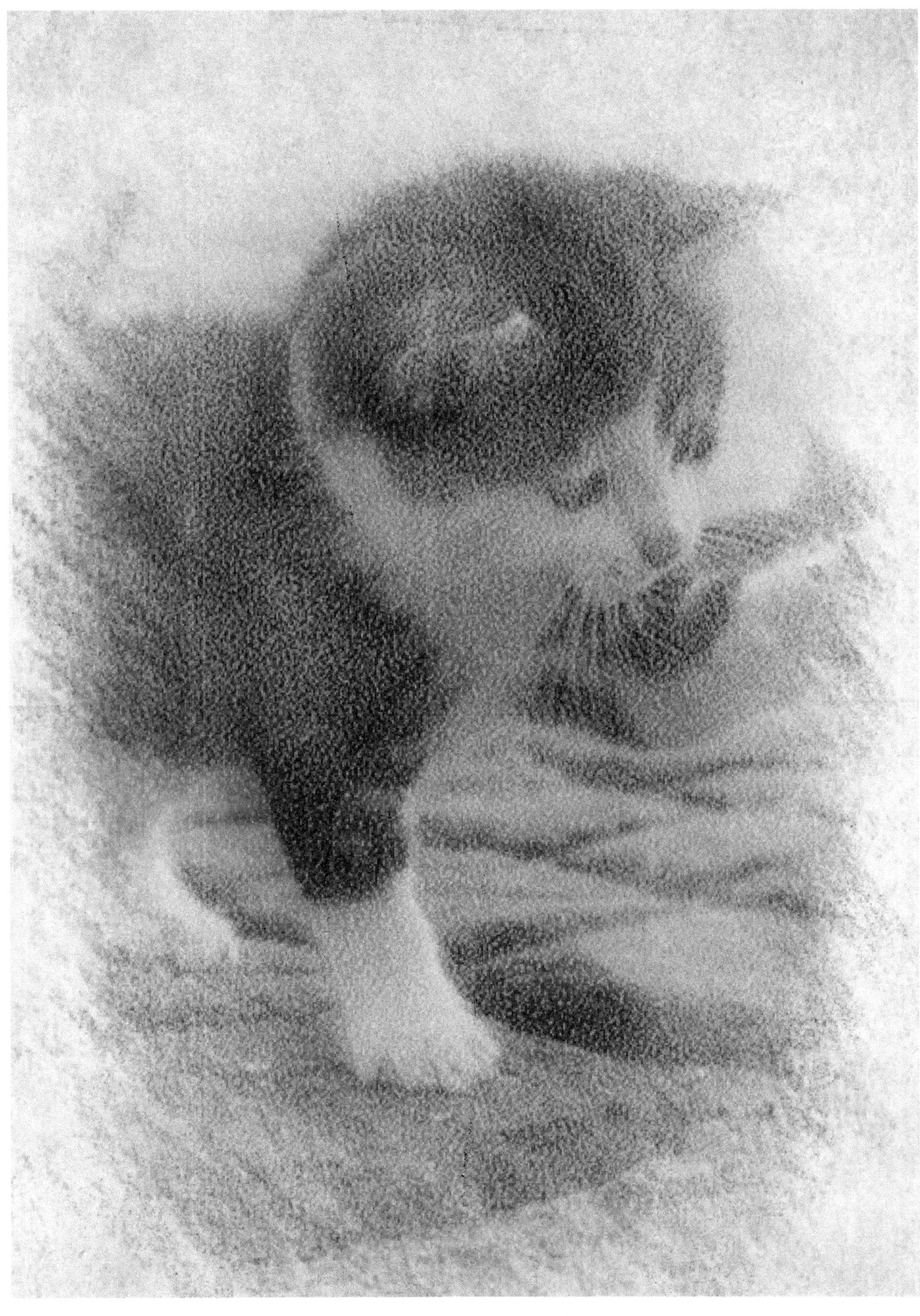

From Frame

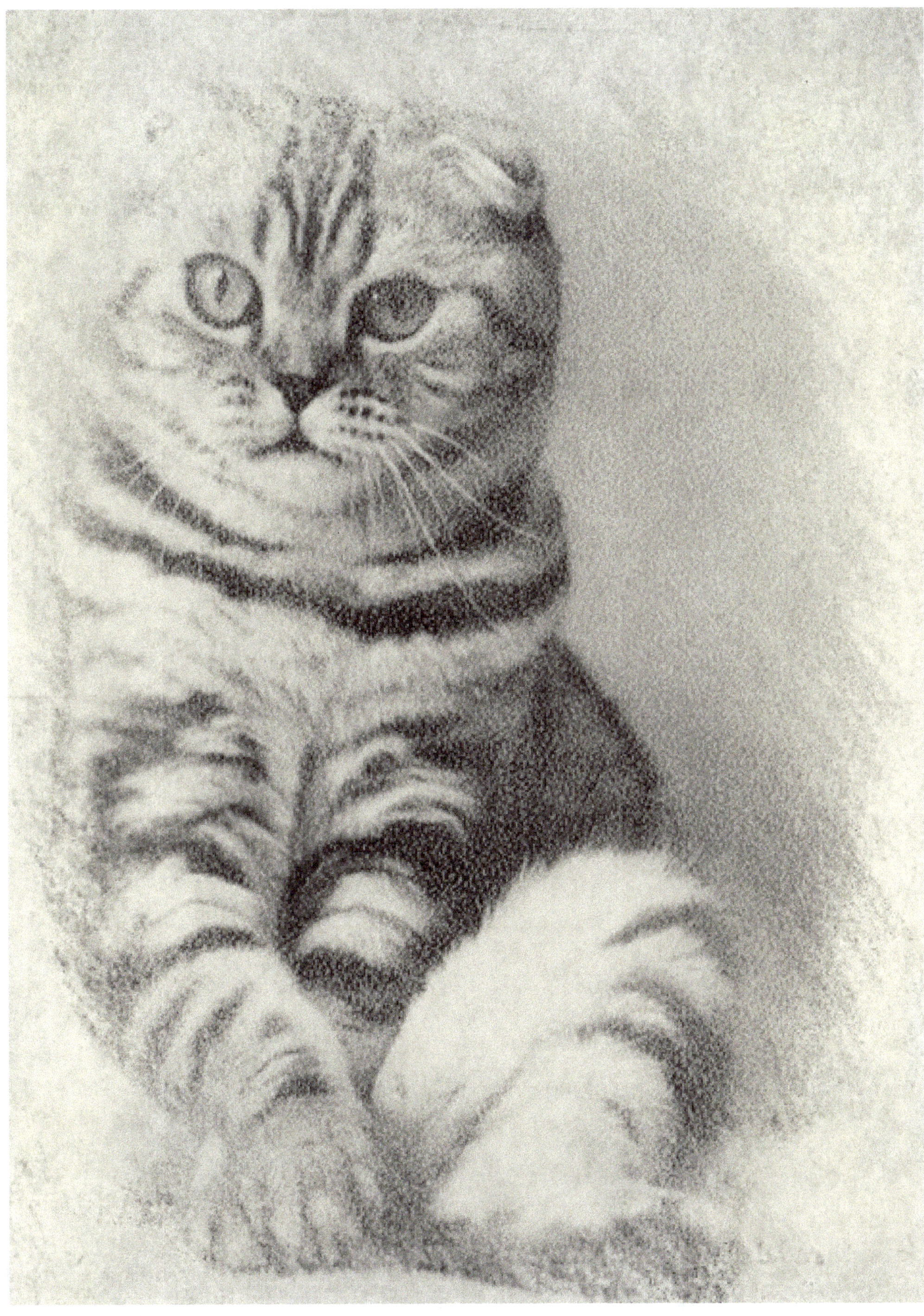

From Frame

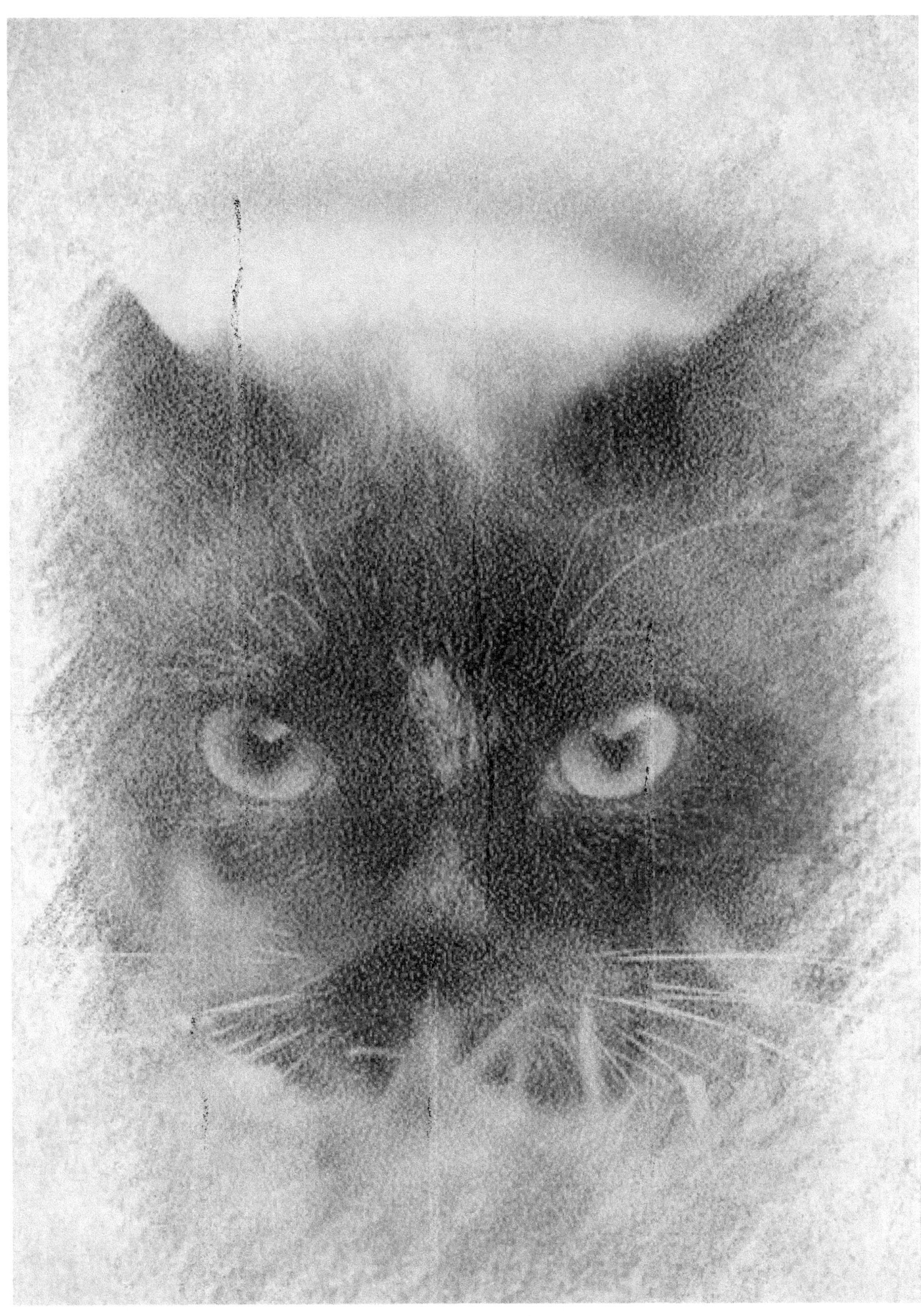

From Frame

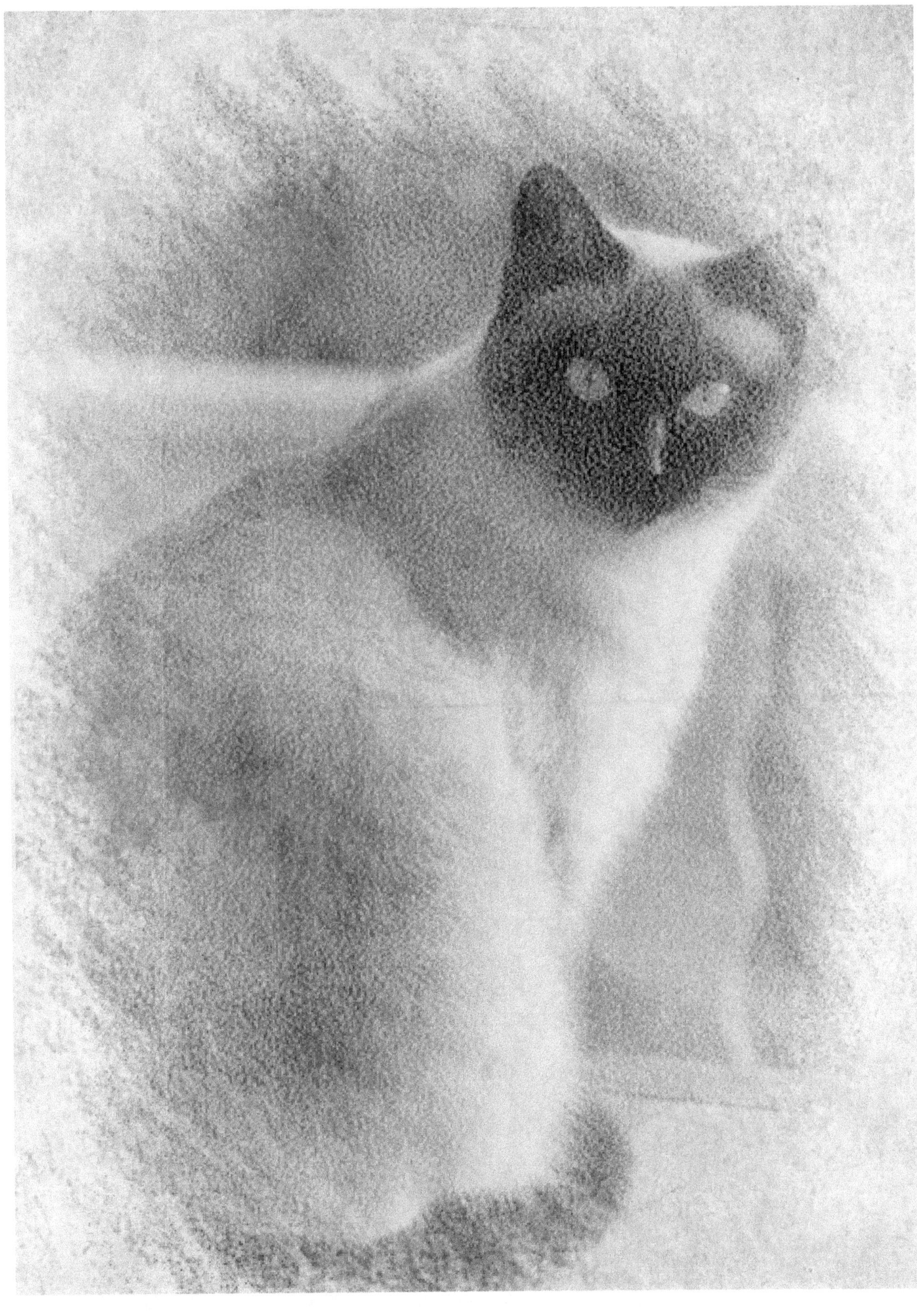

From Frame

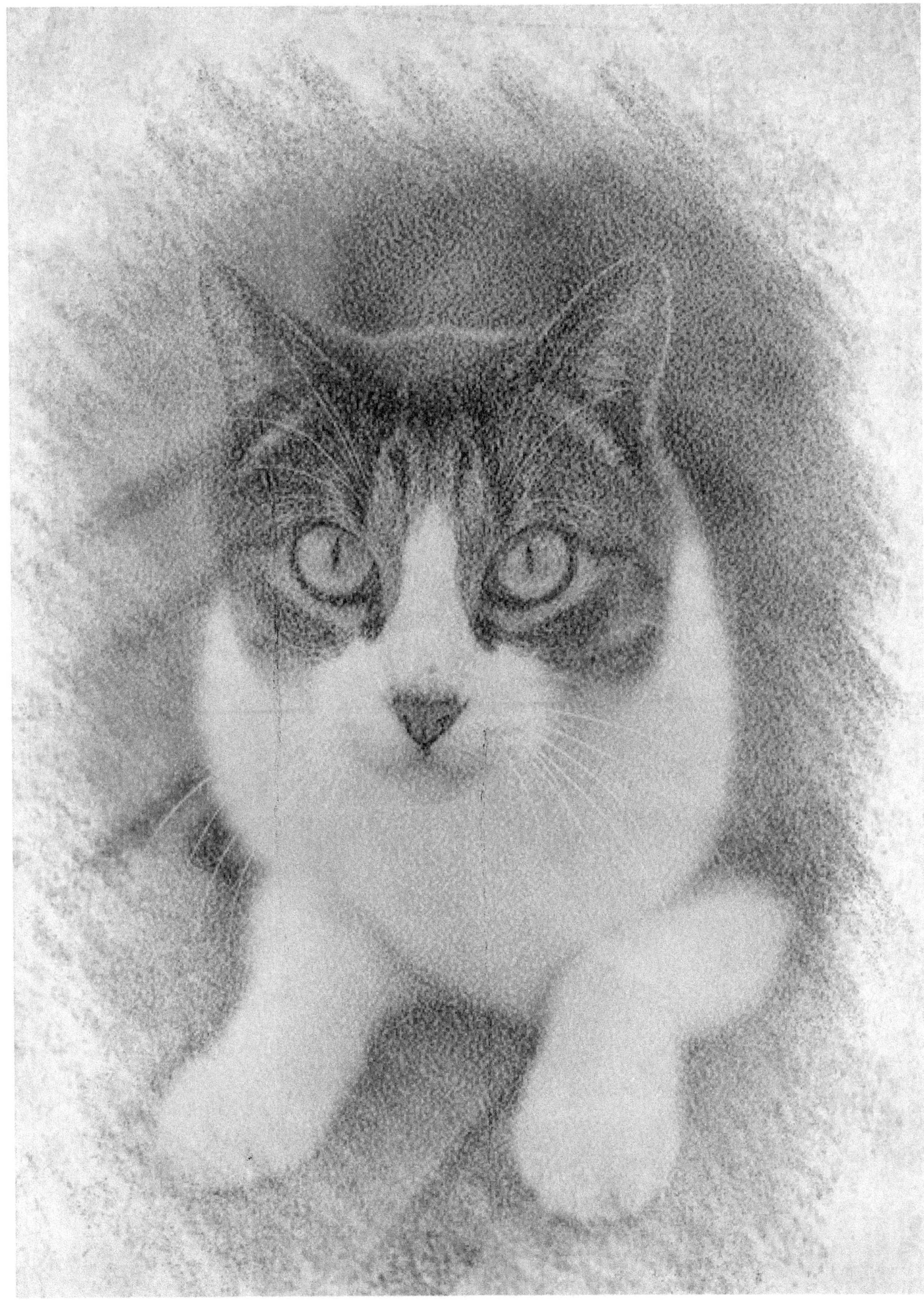

From Frame

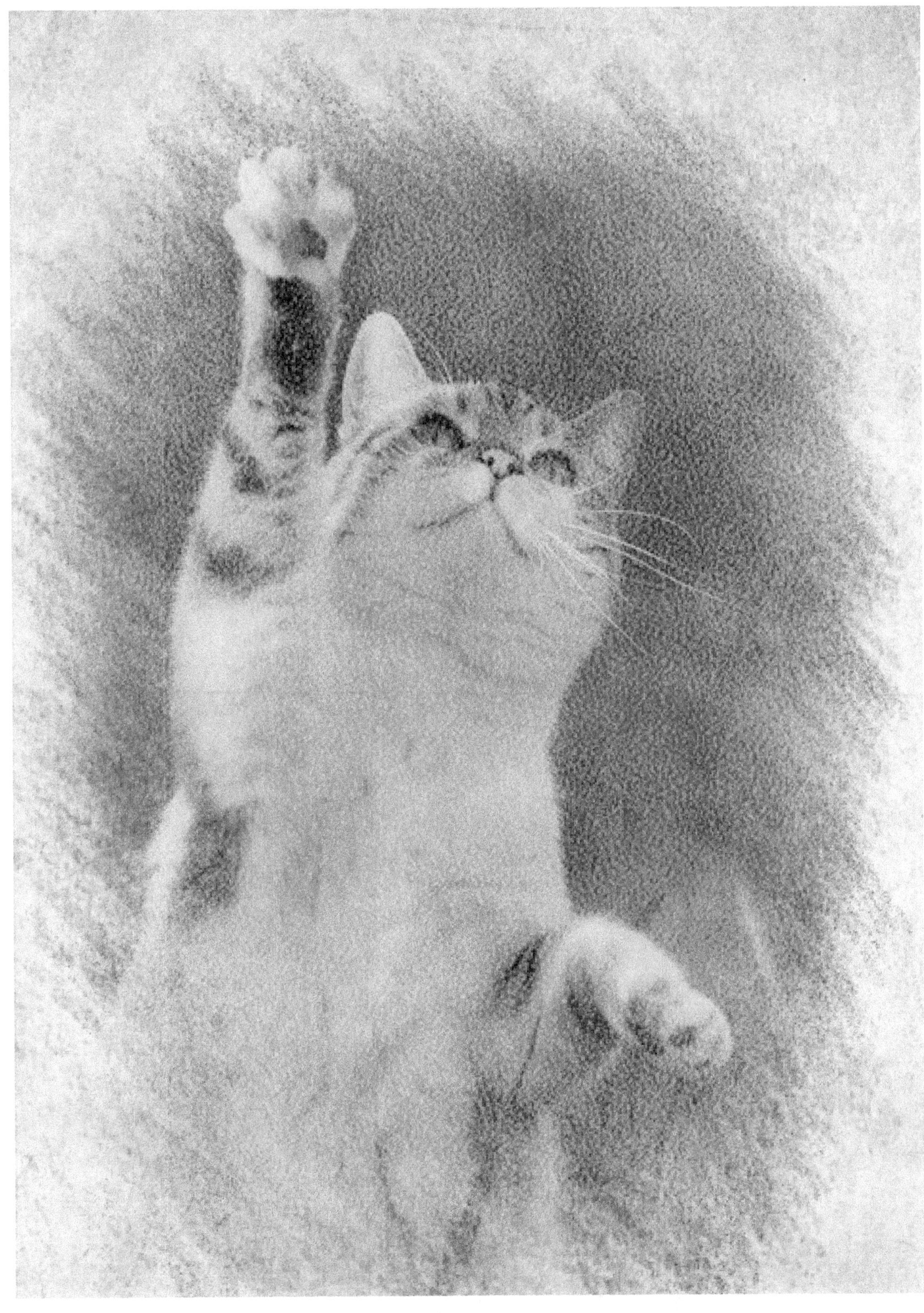

From Frame

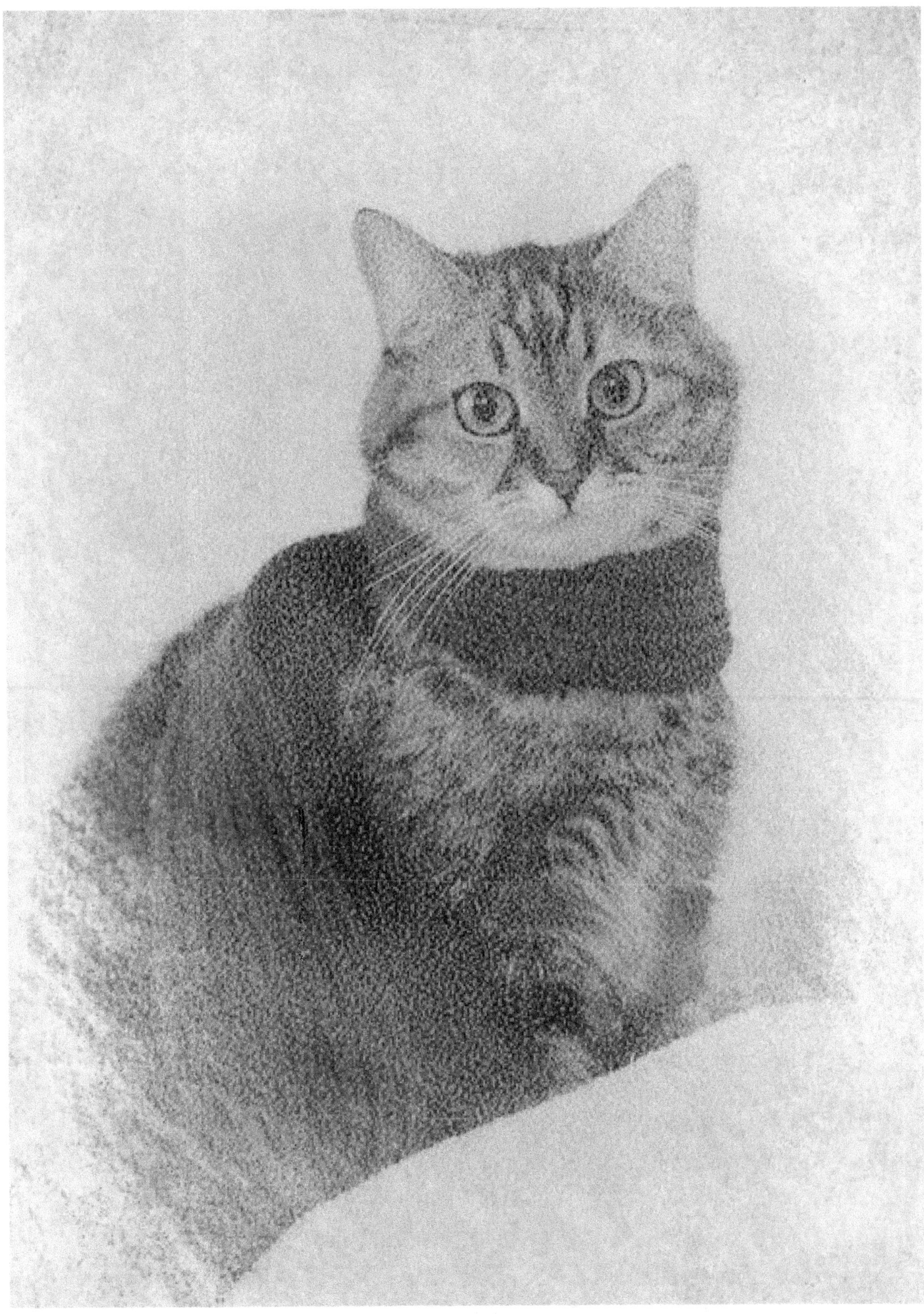

From Frame

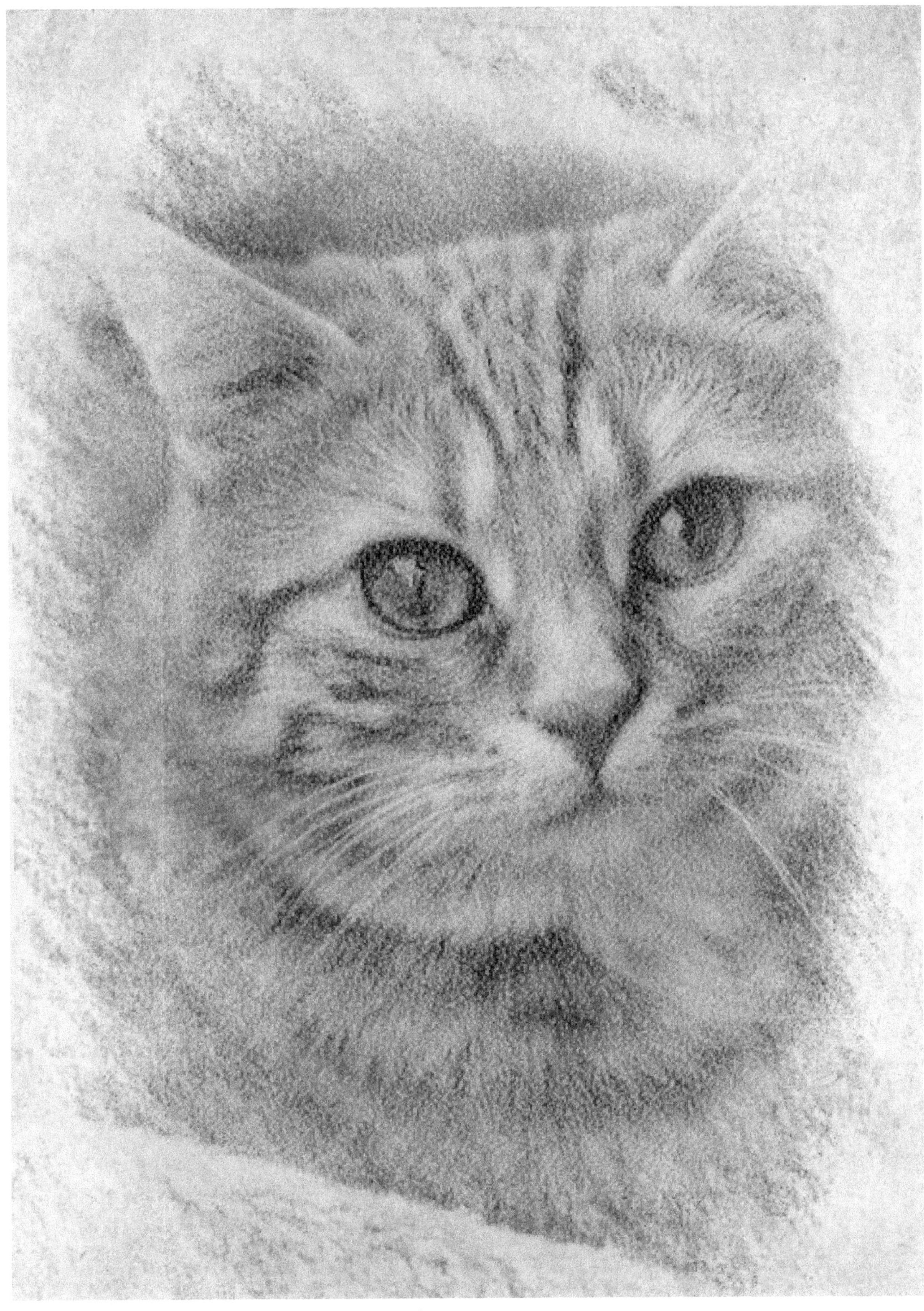

From Frame

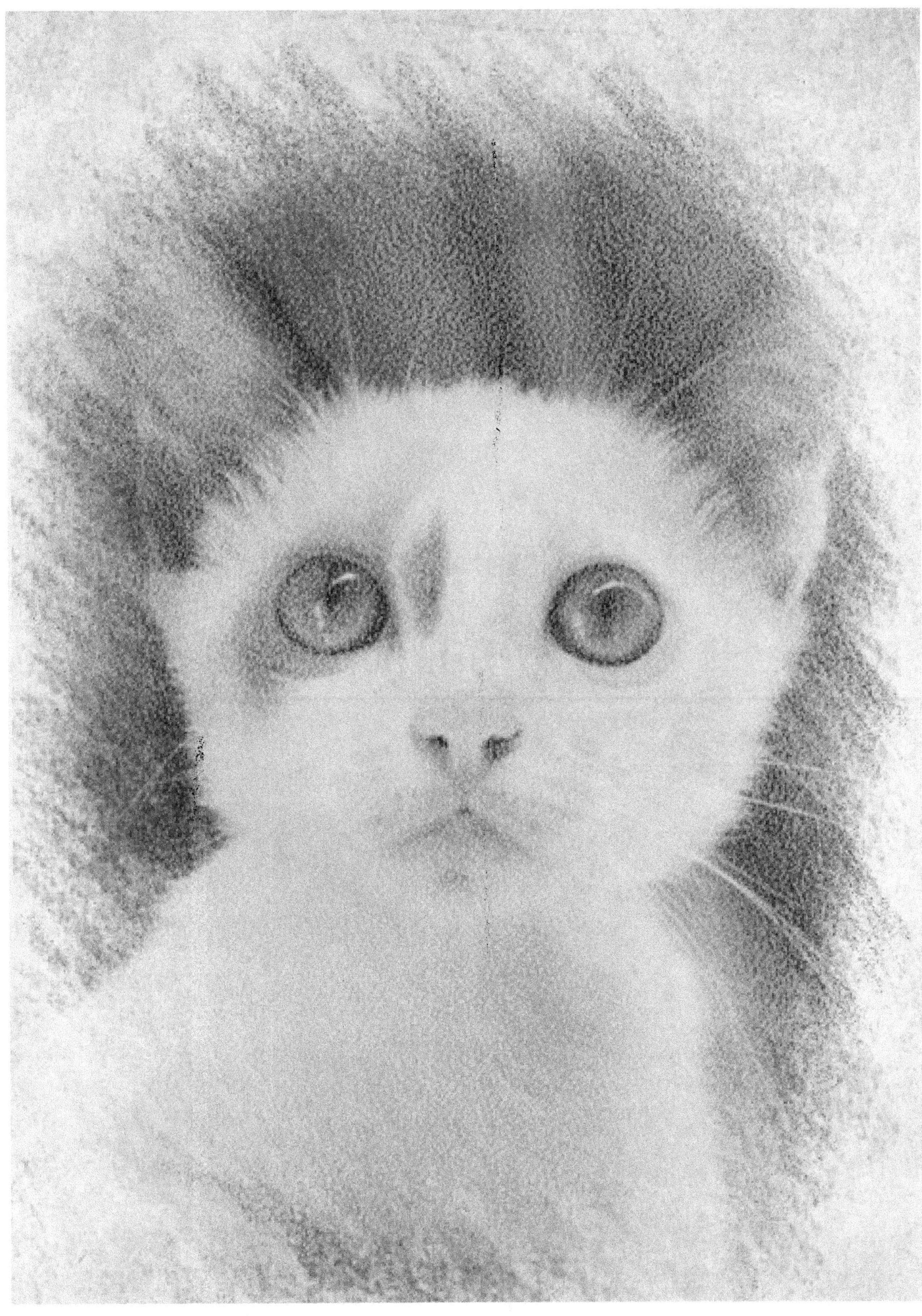

From Frame

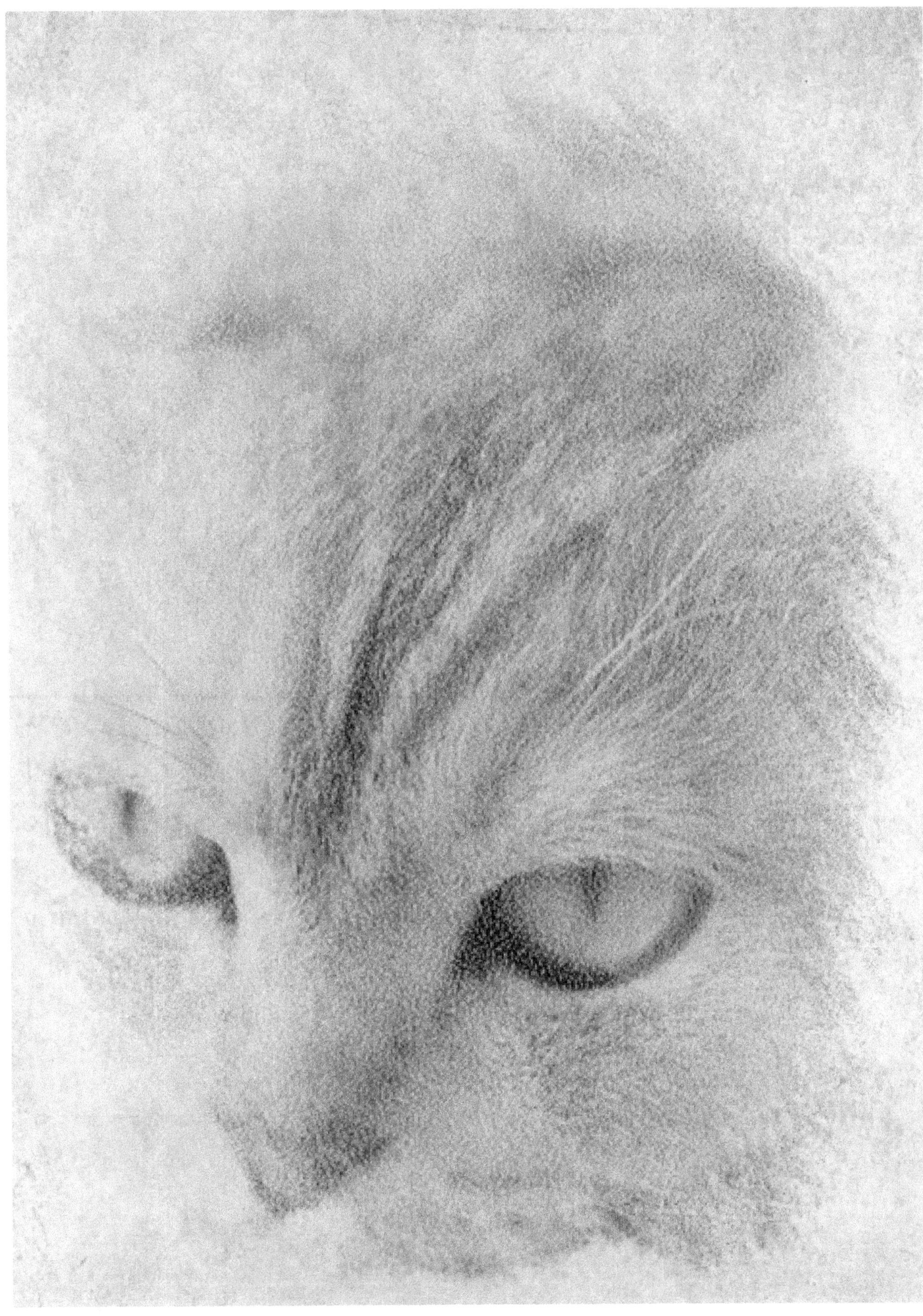

From Frame

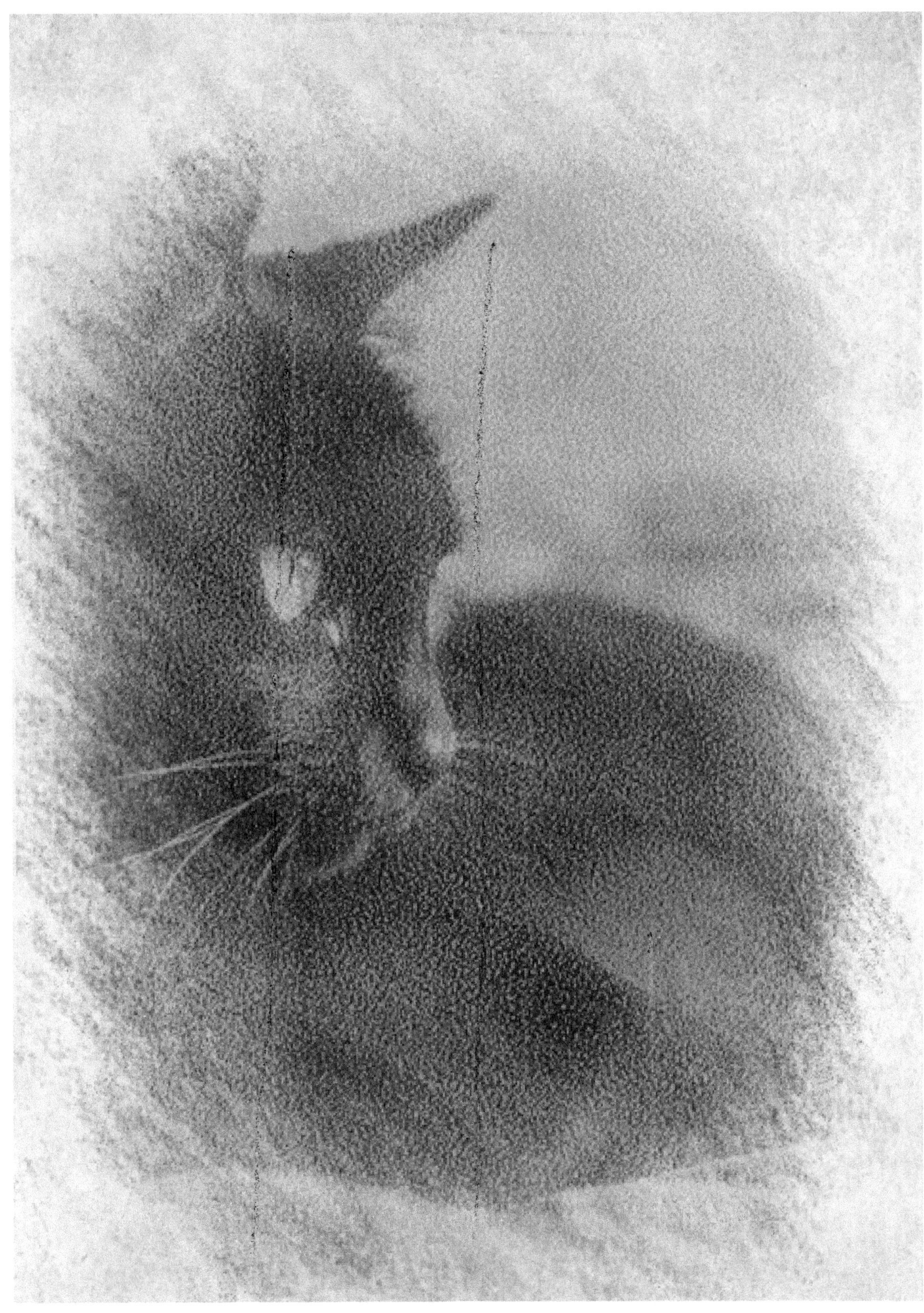

From Frame

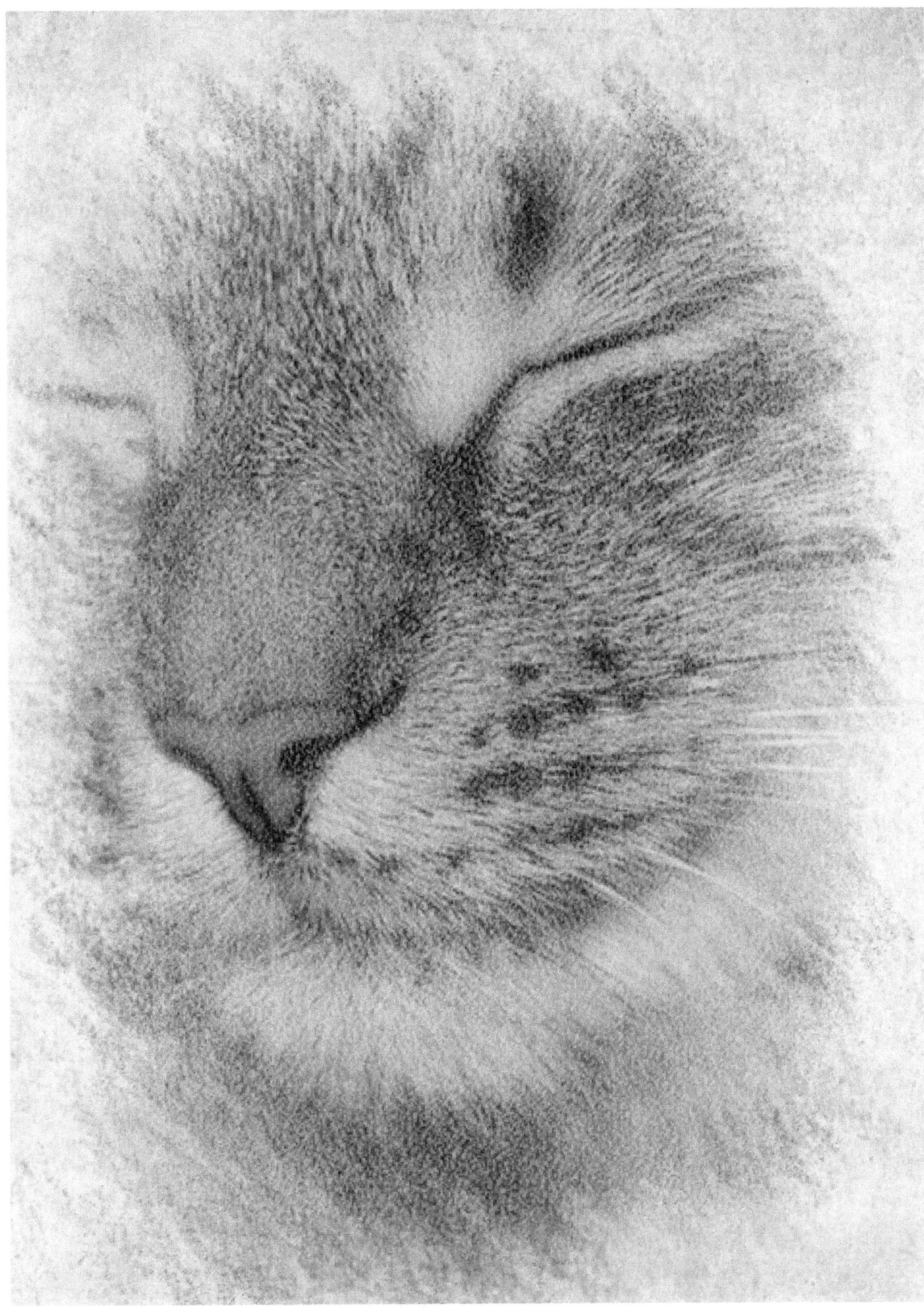

From Frame

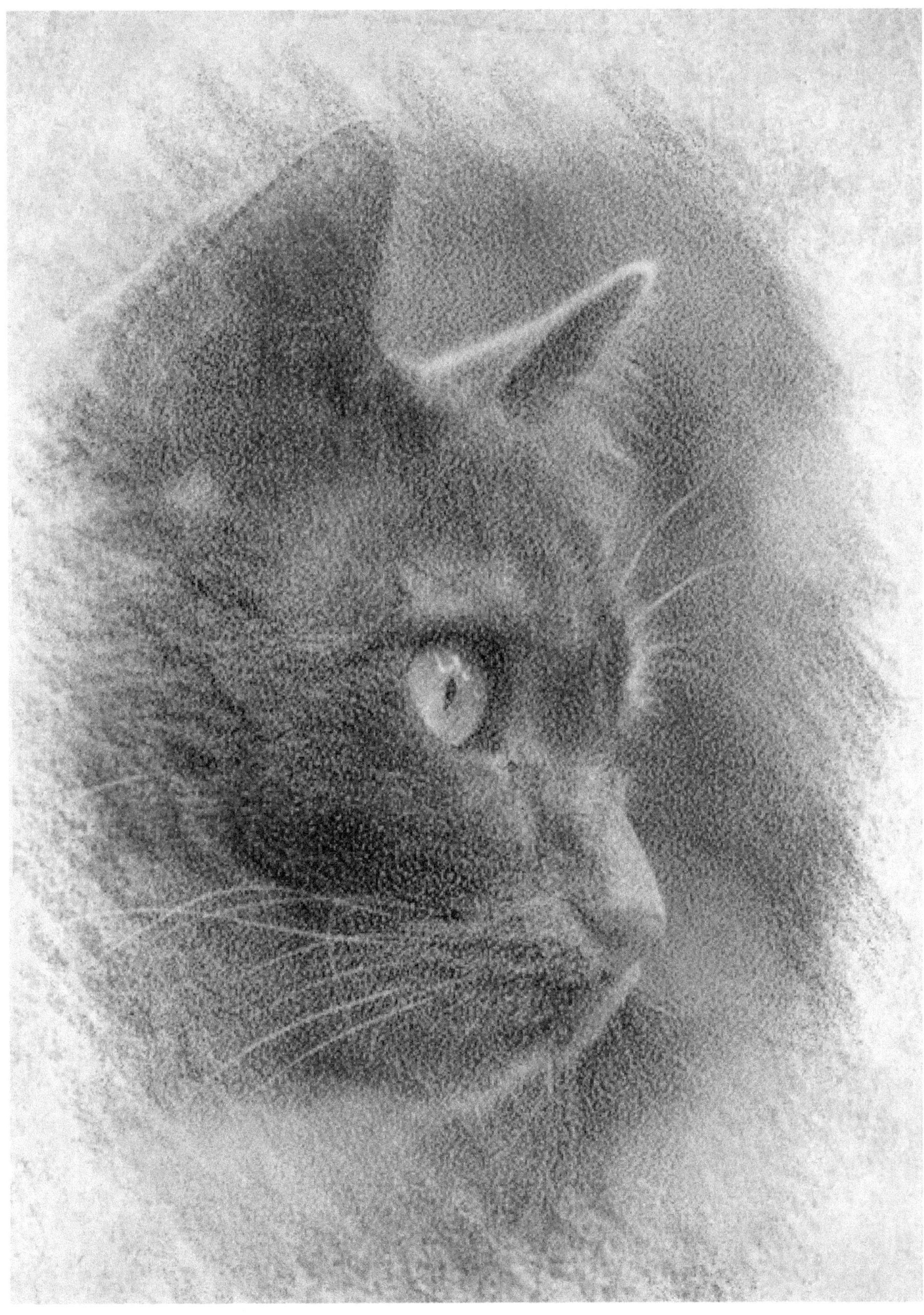

From Frame

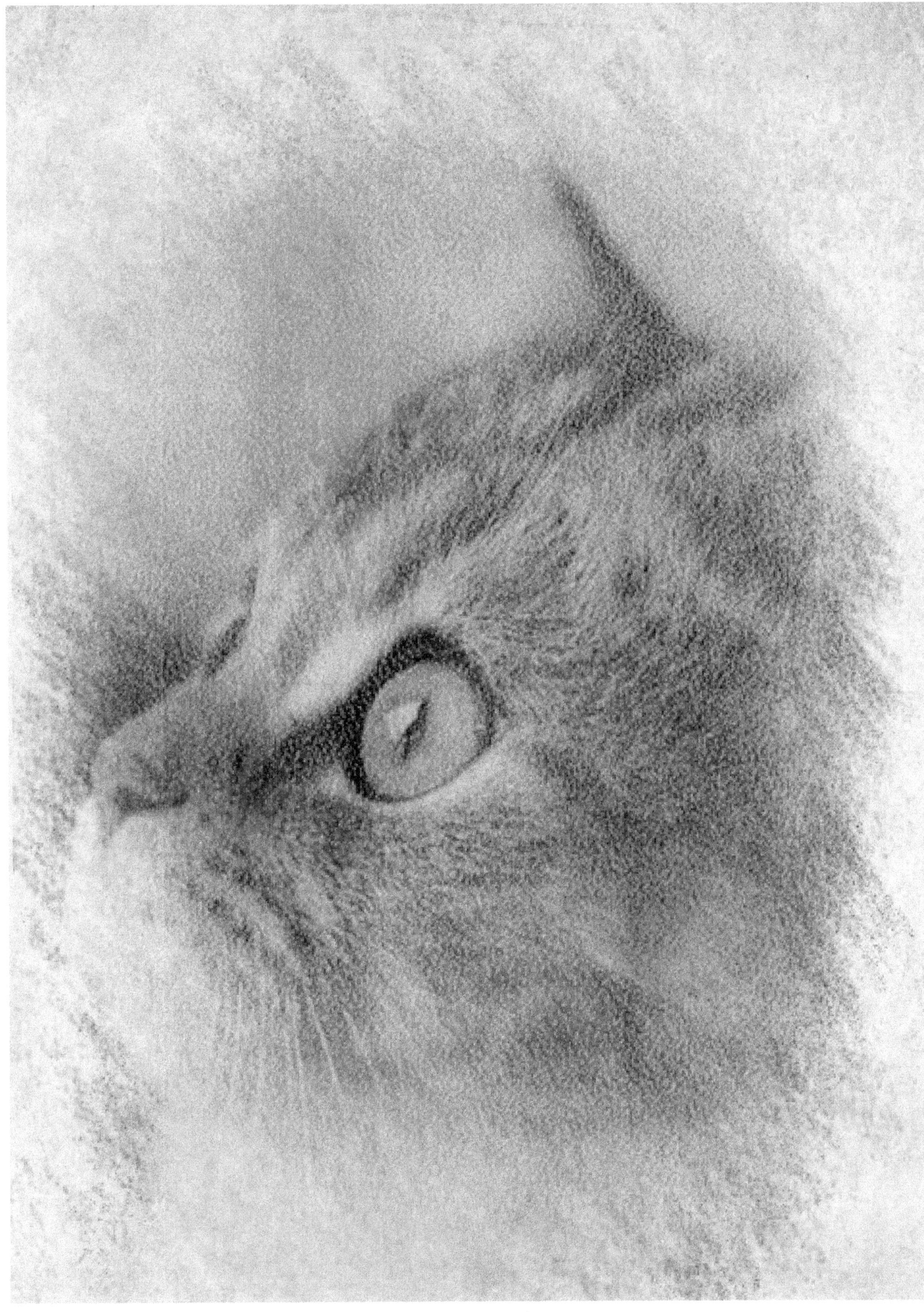

From Frame

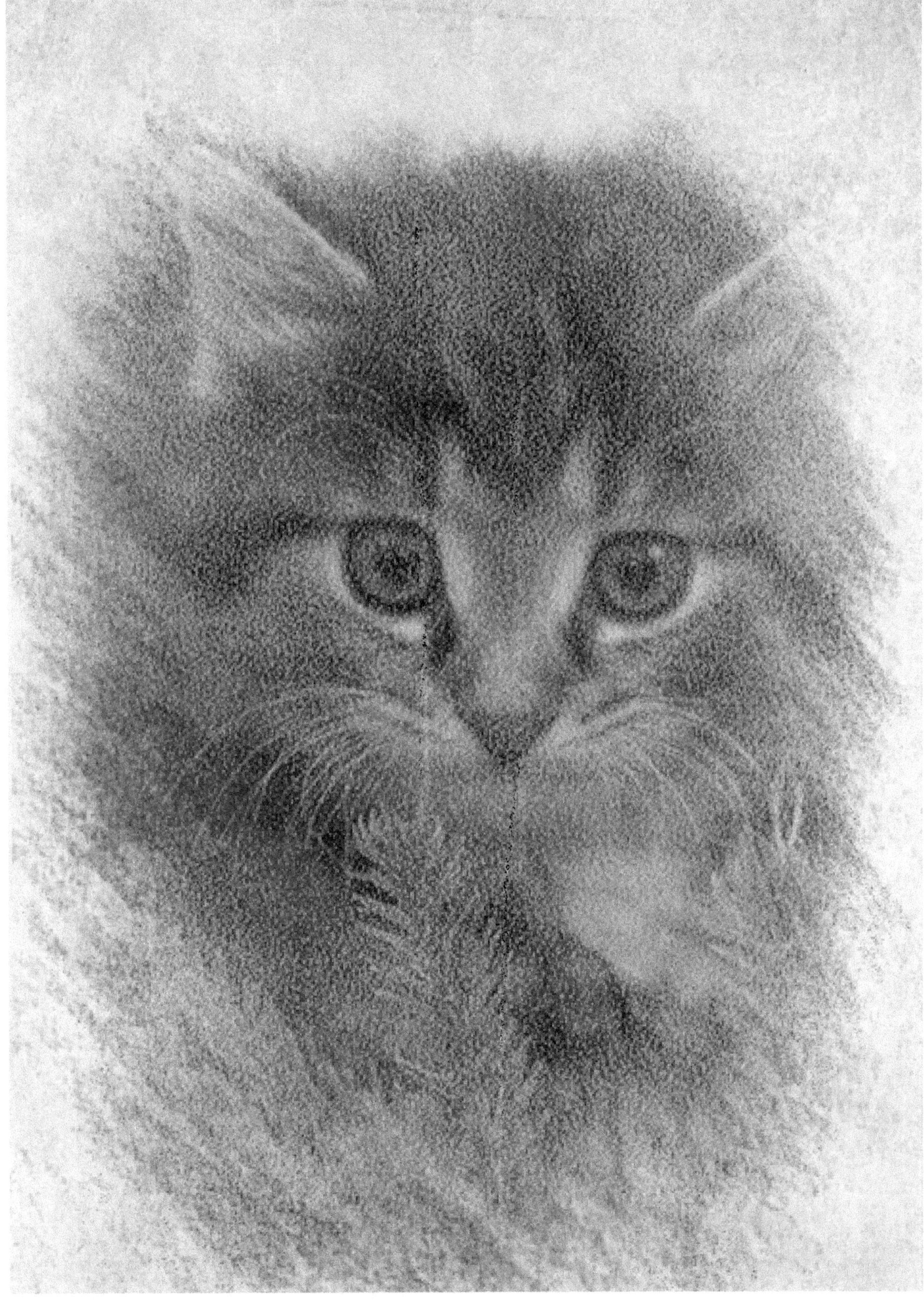

From Frame

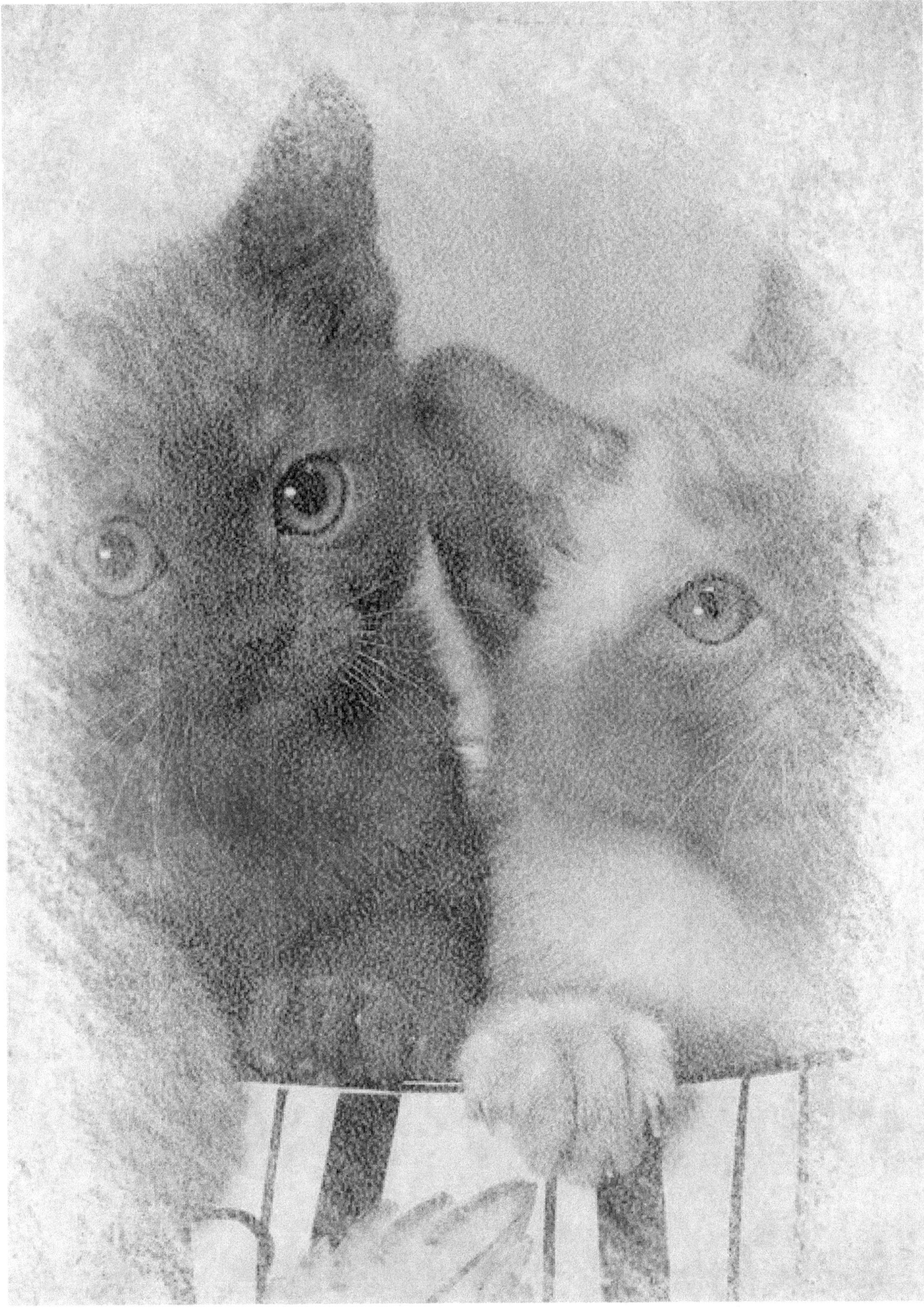

From Frame

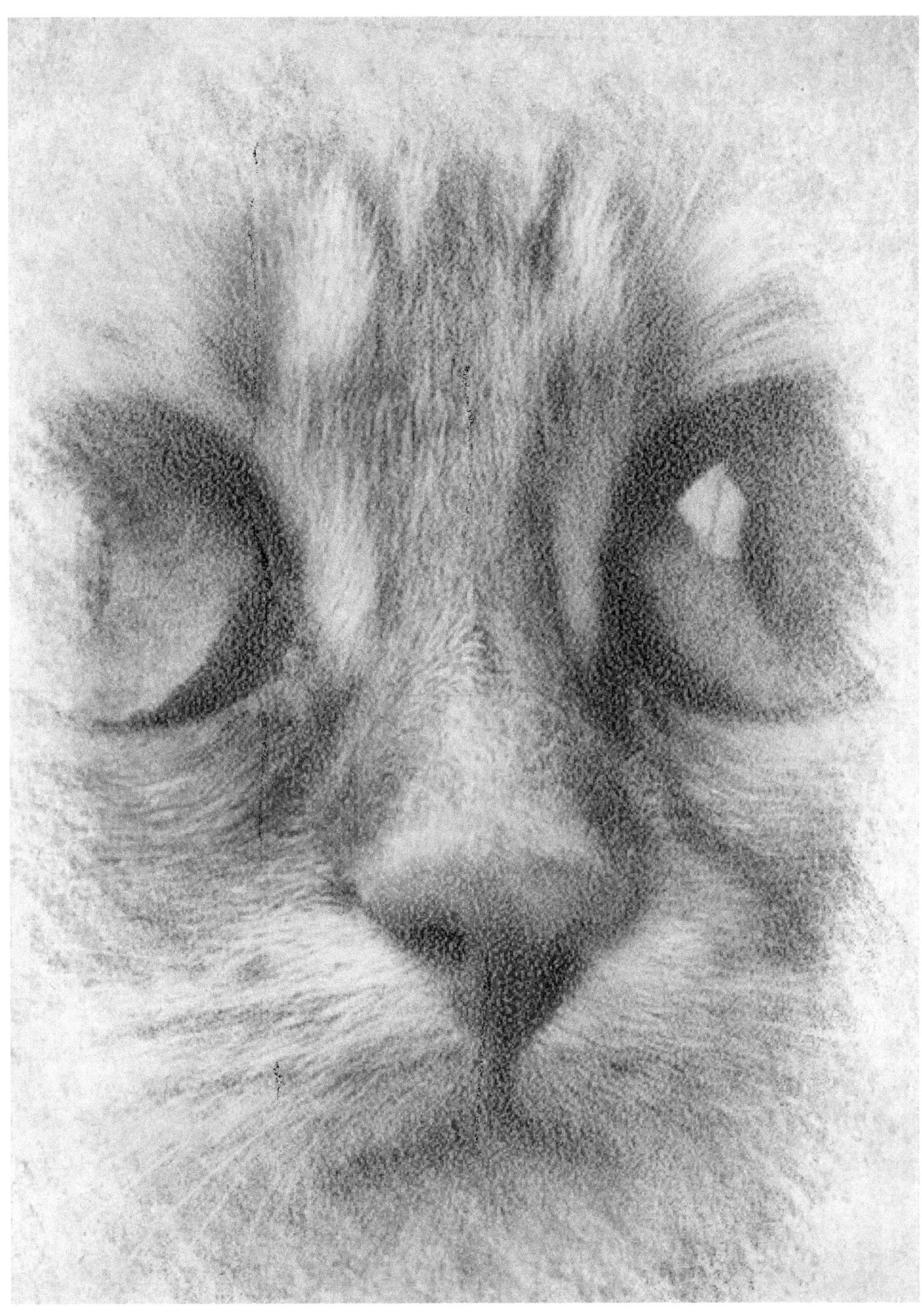

From Frame

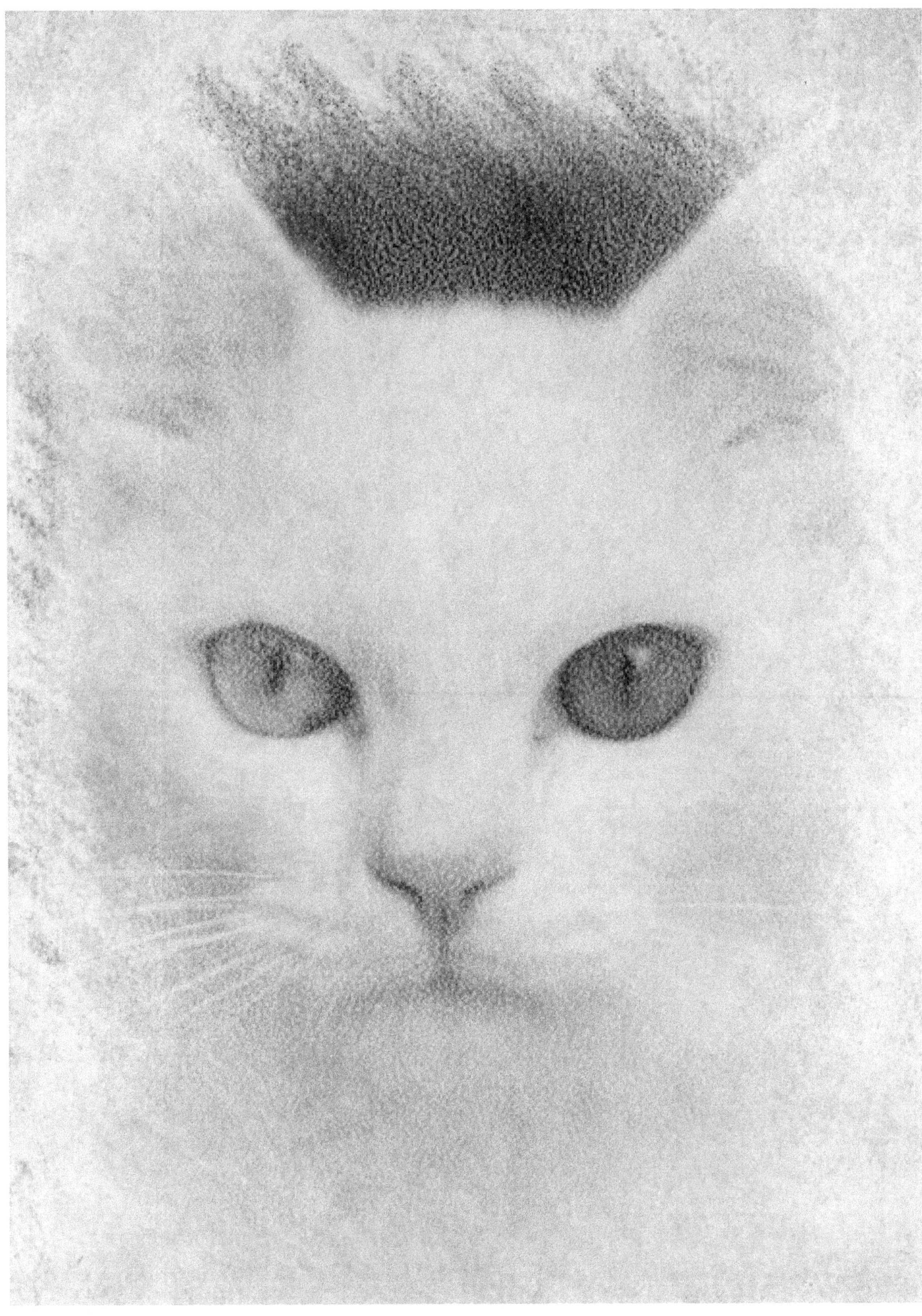

From Frame

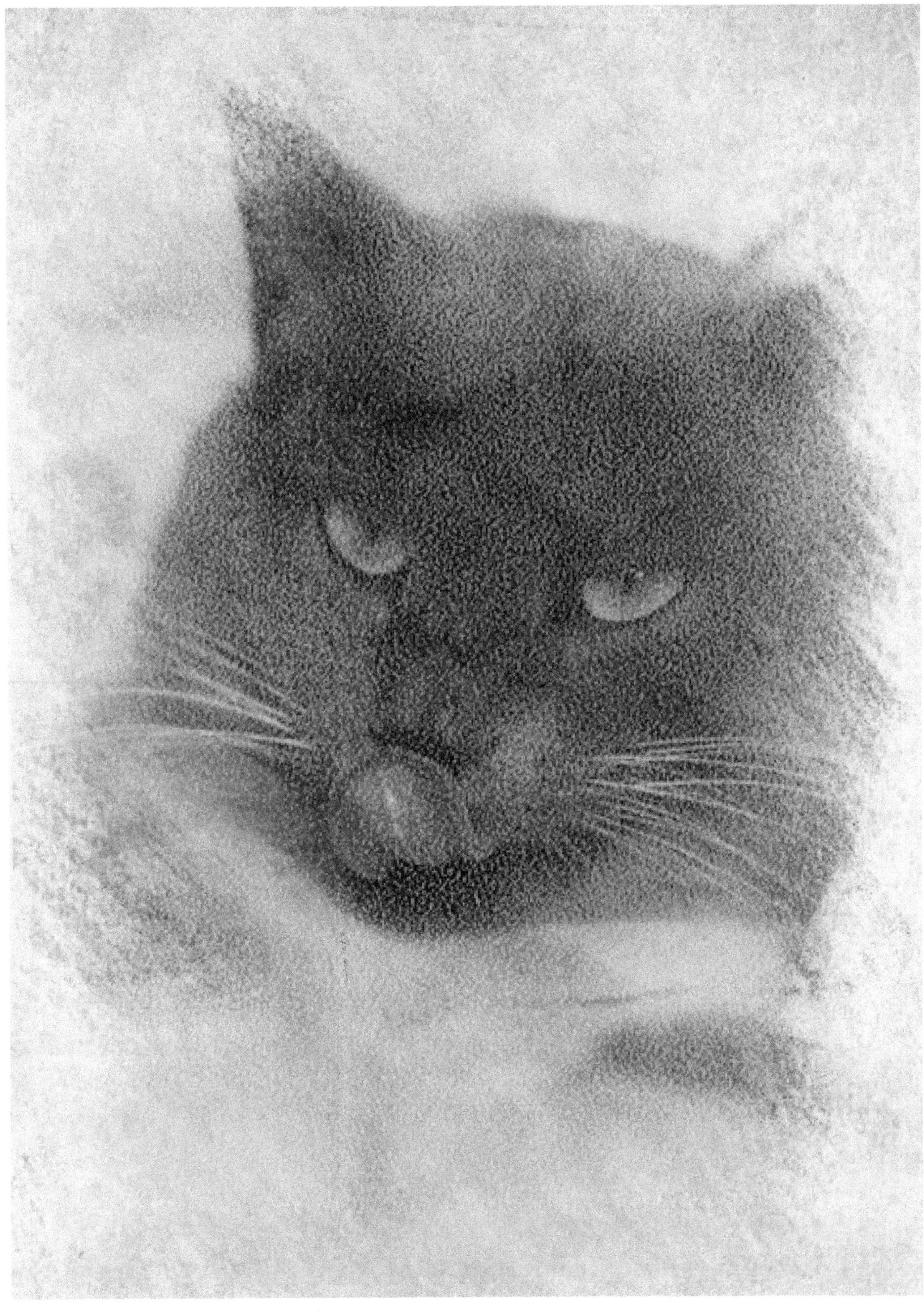

From Frame

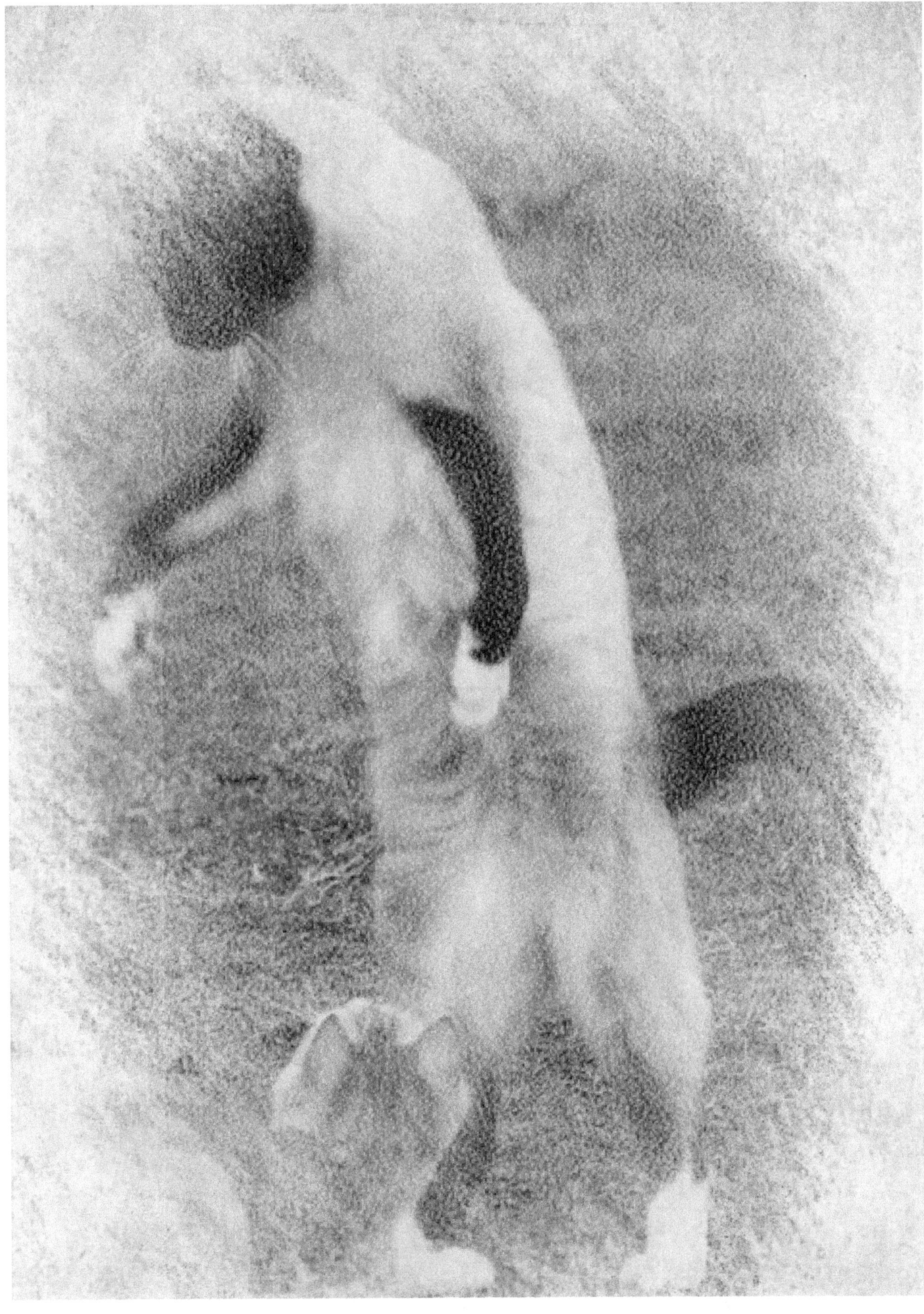

From Frame